T0064885

Quadrant Life™

Balancing Relationships, Finances, Wellness, and Your Spiritual Life

LORI DENNIS

Foreword by Farah Merhi

ALLWORTH PRESS
NEW YORK

Allworth Press books may be purchased in bulk at special discounts for sales promotion, corporate gifts, fund-raising, or educational purposes. Special editions can also be created to specifications. For details, contact the Special Sales Department, Allworth Press, 307 West 36th Street, 11th Floor, New York, NY 10018 or info@skyhorsepublishing.com.

24 23 22 21 20   5 4 3 2 1

Published by Allworth Press, an imprint of Skyhorse Publishing, Inc. 307 West 36th Street, 11th Floor, New York, NY 10018. Allworth Press® is a registered trademark of Skyhorse Publishing, Inc.®, a Delaware corporation.

www.allworth.com

Jacket design by Mary Ann Smith
Jacket photograph provided by Lori Dennis

Library of Congress Cataloging-in-Publication Data
Names: Dennis, Lori, author.
Title: Quadrant life: balancing relationships, finances, wellness, and
    your spiritual life / Lori Dennis.
Description: New York: Allworth Press, [2020]
Identifiers: LCCN 2019050338 (print) | LCCN 2019050339 (ebook) | ISBN
    9781621537441 (hardcover) | ISBN 9781621537458 (epub)
Subjects: LCSH: Happiness. | Quality of life. | Relationship quality. |
    Finance, Personal. | Health. | Religious life.
Classification: LCC BF575.H27 D46 2020 (print) | LCC BF575.H27 (ebook) |
    DDC 646.7—dc23
LC record available at https://lccn.loc.gov/2019050338
LC ebook record available at https://lccn.loc.gov/2019050339

Print ISBN: 978-1-62153-744-1
eBook ISBN: 978-1-62153-745-8

Printed in the United States of America

Contents

Foreword

My name is Farah Merhi. I started Inspire Me! Home Décor back in 2012 as a creative outlet during a time in my life when I felt lost. I didn't know what my purpose in life was, and although I had two kids at the time and an amazing husband, I felt like I still needed something to call my own that truly made me happy.

I was in school working towards my political science degree and getting ready to apply to law school. Three semesters short of graduating, I decided I was quite literally miserable with my career choice. I couldn't bear to spend one more day going through the motions of something I clearly wasn't meant to do.

Inspire Me! became my outlet and my escape as I posted pictures of things that inspired me and of my home. It became apparent to me that home décor is my passion, and I wanted to immerse myself in it fully. People thought I was crazy to leave behind a career that would give me stability and embark into the unknown.

I'll admit it was scary, but I had a vision of what I wanted to do with myself. I knew I had to believe in myself first, or else I wouldn't make it. I took a chance and embarked on this journey, working hard to make sure I would become a success story. I knew I had to at least try and see where it would take me. I owed myself that much. If it didn't work, at least I could say I tried!

Now that I look back, I am thankful that I chose to take that one step out of my fear bubble. I don't mean to say my journey was free of falls and failures, but they made the successes that much sweeter to enjoy.

I was able to move into this unknown territory because I had a very strong bond with my family. With a healthy Relationship Quadrant, I knew that I could depend on them to cheer me on and offer support when things became overwhelming or challenging. Having a solid foundation in my Finance Quadrant allowed me to venture into what ultimately became not only an equally or even more lucrative, but also a much more satisfying business than practicing law. Along the journey, I have built a community of like-minded people who share their successes with each other every day, which fuels my Spirituality and Wellness Quadrants. By reading and following the steps in *Quadrant Life*, you can do the same.

If you're to take anything from my story, it is that life is too short to let fear and other's opinions hold you back. Take control of your own destiny. With hard work, passion, drive, and dedication, everything and anything is possible. You owe yourself that much.

—Farah Merhi
December 2019

Introduction

If you're looking for a happy and successful life, you've picked the right book. I'm standing at the top of Happy Mountain, looking down on the path to this magnificent place, and I can't wait to share my road map with you. Writing this book is one of the ways I plan to pay it forward in the hopes that what I've learned will open your eyes and help you experience a life of fulfillment.

I am madly in love with my husband, I have a phenomenal kid, my friendships are sincere, I perform meaningful work that has made me wealthy, I'm full of energy, I never get sick, and I am connected to my creator. But it wasn't always like that for me. It took many setbacks and quite a few years to achieve nirvana in my life.

Trying to find happiness and prosperity, I studied many books and people I admired, attended seminars, and even spent thousands of dollars in therapy. Along the way, I picked up nuggets and gems of wisdom in my quest, but for many years my life still wasn't in sync.

My relationships were tumultuous, and I eventually went through a divorce. Work was hard and unsatisfying. The friends I had chosen to spend time with were chaotic. A feeling of sadness was always with me. I wondered what I was doing wrong and thought that maybe I was just dealt bad cards. Maybe you're thinking that way too.

I made a decision and I declared it to the Universe: "I am ready to be happy now and I am willing to take full responsibility for my life." Then it finally clicked. Everything in my life started to move in the right direction.

THE FOUR QUADRANTS

I have experienced what it takes to find happiness and success. It's not a secret, and you won't get it by just thinking great thoughts. The reality is that it takes effort and the knowledge of how to balance the four areas that impact your life the most: relationships, finances, wellness, and spirituality.

These four parts overlap each other throughout your existence, and when they are in harmony, you thrive. Your life becomes a state of flow and possibility where everything feels more natural. When your life is in balance, you don't worry as much. You sleep better. You're unafraid. You notice that you're frequently smiling and you have more to give to others. On the flip side, when you neglect one of these areas, your life quality suffers.

Do you ever look at people who have all the things you want and think, "How come I don't live that way? I'm just as smart, talented, and good looking as they are!" It's because you're lacking in one (or more) areas of your life. When your life is balanced, the path to joy and abundance becomes clear and obtainable. When you're in alignment, you transform from a state of "just existing" to prosperity and purpose. The days stop blending into each other, and you stop wondering, "Is this all there is?"

These quadrants of your life are universal, and they have always affected humans. Early humans relied on relationships to procreate before verbal language was even invented; finance boiled down to establishing a food source; wellness meant staying alive by avoiding danger; and our quest for something more significant is to this very day is the essence of spirituality and how all religions and philosophies came to be.

Now that most of our basic needs are met, our quest is no longer about simply surviving. Today we hunt for happiness, success, and purpose. Yet the same four aspects of our life hold equal importance on our journey.

GET HAPPY

Deciding to be happy is a choice that you must make, and it's one you must continue to make every day. It requires practice and determination, just like learning to play an instrument or learning a new language.

Reading this book will show you how to build strength and achieve harmony in your four areas, which gives you the stamina to keep moving ahead. Everyone experiences feelings of fear and loneliness, like nothing we do is any good and nothing really matters.

Some people know how to pass through these moments of feeling blue; others stay stuck for way too long. Which one are you? What kind of life do you want?

Are you ready to take responsibility for your actions, stop blaming others, get into balance, and make progress? Because when you pay attention to the quadrants and nurture your relationships, finances, wellness, and spirituality, you will establish a joyful and rewarding life.

Almost Having It All

If you are not happy, it's time to ask yourself why and address the parts of your life that need work. What's been getting in the way of your happiness until now? What part of your life is being neglected or missing altogether?

I had an interior design client who was killing it at work. She's married to a smoking hot partner and they have a loving relationship. But she was always tired and unhappy. She drank about six cups of coffee to get through the day and worked her ass off—one time she even went into work so sick, she barfed in the parking lot and just kept on going.

Every night she came home and drank a bottle of wine to quiet the noise. She went to bed buzzed and confessed that sometimes she didn't even brush her teeth. Her sleep was no good and she woke up throughout the night. She had a slight headache every morning and was exhausted, but she started right back up the next day with a cup of coffee and repeated the same thing all over.

She knew it wasn't healthy and she was unhappy, yet she never changed. At what point do you ask yourself, why am I doing this? What am I missing and how do I achieve balance?

Finances and Relationships are overpowering Wellness and Spirituality in her situation, and even though she's rich and happily married, she's miserable. Until you even out these four areas, you remain in a state of want, no matter how great your relationship is and how much money you make. You will not be happy until you balance the four areas of your life.

But He's a Yoga Teacher

One of my yoga teachers is very enlightened; he is the one who shows everyone how to be mentally flexible, spiritual, patient, and loving to each other. He was a champion gymnast, so he can do all kinds of impressive things with his body. He's also really handsome, so his classes are packed and he's succeeding financially. His life is all about doing well by helping others. You can see he's truly inspired by watching his students bloom.

He's always a little sad when I talk to him outside of class, because his relationships are not working out as well as the other parts of his life. He never picks appropriate romantic partners and he's always disappointed in his relationships. They don't work and they don't last.

I wonder why someone who is so spiritually successful isn't working more on the relationship part of his life. And that's exactly my point. We can be great at two or three areas of our life, but you're going to have to examine where you are weak and work on that part if you want to thrive.

These are just a few examples of people who look like they have it all together, but don't. To the rest of the world, they look like they're succeeding, but they're not fulfilling their potential and it makes them unhappy.

We each have our own circumstance; each journey is different, but the principle is the same throughout time, religion, gender, and society. You have to balance the four quadrants if you want to be happy.

PART ONE: RELATIONSHIPS

The book begins with looking at all of our relationships, not just romantic ones. We will dive into some of the most challenging questions of how we relate to others and we will discover new and productive ways to let go, grow, and evolve emotionally.

How is your emotional past affecting your present? Are you repeating patterns that you learned and ending up feeling disappointed? How do you put the past in the past and move forward? What kind of connections do you have to family, friends, your spouse, your kids, and other people in your life?

Do these experiences enrich your life or leave you feeling drained? What does your love life look like? You also have a relationship with the space you inhabit. What does your home say about you, and is it bringing security or stress? By identifying these problems, we can work toward the solutions and create harmony in our relationships.

PART TWO: FINANCES

In the Finance chapters we probe into issues involving money, career, consumerism, and debt. This is where we learn about investment strategies that everyone should know. Are you using money as tool to increase the quality of your life? Or is it being used against you like a weapon? Do you have a plan for financial freedom? What are your thoughts about money?

Are you satisfied with your work? Does what you do for a living help you to have meaning in your life? Are you going into debt by trying to buy happiness? We will work on action plans to help you get out of debt and, more importantly, analyze the reason you got there in the first place. We'll shed light on how finances affect your life and how to gain control.

PART THREE: WELLNESS

If you don't have your health, the rest of the quadrants don't really matter. In the Wellness chapters we dive into diet, fitness, stress reduction, and rejuvenation. Your body is your vessel to move through life—it's critical you learn how it works and how to maintain it properly.

How does what we eat affect our brain and body chemistry? Are you addicted to sugar, and how do you break the habit? How do you prevent degenerative diseases? We will look at ways to grow new brain cells.

How does sitting all day affect your wellness? What types of exercise help to slow the aging process? Do you want to master techniques for managing stress and extending your life?

Wellness is about so much more than going on a diet and hitting the gym.

PART FOUR: SPIRITUALITY

In the last few chapters, we examine spirituality, which includes meditation, the law of attraction, connection to community, and the negative power of fear. This section is often overlooked or dismissed by most people as less important than the other quadrants. Because it's not tangible like holding hands with someone, having money, or being fit, it's hard to understand the value.

People spend their lives building strength in relationships, finances, and wellness, yet they still feel afraid and stuck for the majority of their lives. Many people don't discover the peace that spirituality brings until later in life, when they feel they finally have the time and luxury to reflect or give back to others. In this final quadrant, we will demystify the ideas of spirituality. We will identify how to benefit from being in a state of awareness, possibility, love, and gratitude.

Once you understand the basic principles of these four impactful quadrants of your life, you'll have the power to get them into balance. Being in this place of parity—mentally, financially, physically, and spiritually—gives you the confidence to accept and overcome the many challenges you encounter each day. Self-doubt and fear then appear only as infrequent visitors, while happiness and gratitude become your new best friends.

WINNING EVERY DAY

It's intimidating to try to change your entire life all at once. So where do you start? The best way to begin is by making little easy-to-accomplish changes every day in the parts of your life that aren't as strong as the others. Having little wins every day releases endorphins, which are biochemical bursts of happiness in your brain.

These regular bursts of endorphins are addictive. The more you win, the happier you get. You're also conditioning yourself to expect accomplishment. You turn those little moments of wins into big wins, and it becomes a way of life.

I first experienced the joy of little wins with my husband in the beginning of our relationship when we made the bed together in the morning. He was so excited about making the bed every day, with a noticeable smile on his face every time. I liked him a lot, and he was cute, but still, it was weird. Who gets pumped up about making a bed?

He explained that when we made the bed, it was going to be "inviting" at the end of the day when we were ready to get back in it, and that made him happy. In the first few minutes of his day, he was already collecting a win. Now I smile every time I make the bed, and I collect a win too. As you read this book, look for places where you can gain little wins on a daily basis. Or you can just start by making the bed. Now, let's dive in and let the balance begin.

SAVINGS DIET
CHANGING FITNESS
CAREERS
FINANCES WELLNESS
MEANINGFUL STRESS
WORK
CONSUMERISM SELF-CARE
DEBT BALANCE HOME
INVESTMENTS
LAW OF ROMANCE
ATTRACTION EMOTIONAL DNA
SPIRITUALITY FRIENDS
COMMUNITY FAMILY
FEAR LOVE

PART I
RELATIONSHIPS

NO ONE CAN MAKE YOU FEEL INFERIOR

without your consent.

- Eleanor Roosevelt

CHAPTER 1

Emotional DNA

How is your past affecting your present? Many of us live out our lives as victims because of events that occurred in the past. Our history forms our belief systems and the ways we react to present situations.

When your emotional well-being has been compromised by an event or person in your past, it's common to suffer wounds that feel like they will never heal. Once you identify what caused the scar, you can reconcile the feelings that are causing you pain.

PARENTS

Can we blame it on our parents? Some of us grow up with a rage-filled, violent parent, resulting in years of not being able to stand our ground. We never disagree or disappoint for fear of making someone angry. We find ourselves constantly apologizing, even when we know we did nothing wrong. Living a life of compromise to avoid verbal or physical abuse becomes our default. Or else we behave the exact same way to the people we are close to in our lives.

Others have parents who abandoned them or didn't give enough emotional or financial support. This violation of trust can lead to years of flawed relationships, founded on the belief that they don't deserve any better. Intimacy is difficult when you can't trust people.

Maybe your parents were incredibly supportive, kind, and generous, but so controlling (aka helicopters) that you were never able to develop through controversy and learn that you could survive. Or have you heard of the only child syndrome? Is it all about you, being selfish, thinking that you're owed everything and nothing is ever good enough?

SITUATIONAL DAMAGE

Perhaps your childhood was just fine and your parents were lovely, but something awful happened later in your life. What was it that formed your belief system, harming your ability to thrive in the Relationships Quadrant?

- a teacher who humiliated you
- a significant other who cheated on you
- someone who unfairly sued you
- a family member who insulted you
- a business partner who stole from you
- the loss of a business or home
- a large loss in an investment
- an accident or violent assault
- molestation or sexual abuse[1]

---

1   If you have been molested or sexually abused, you should seek professional therapy. If you cannot afford it, research group therapy near you and ask for a sliding-scale payment based on your ability to contribute.

THINGS YOU HEARD

It could be that nothing bad happened to you at all. Instead, your beliefs were formed by listening to the ideas of people you admire. T. Harv Eker talks about this in his book *Secrets of the Millionaire Mind.* We grow up hearing things that turn into our reality, never understanding how these untrue words compromise our ability to succeed in personal or business relationships.

Here are a few gems I recall hearing on a regular basis throughout my life. Any of them sound familiar?

"Life's a bitch, then you die."	Imagine how this sets up your expectations for a joyous existence.
"We can't afford that."	How do you think this limits your aspirations when it comes to being financially secure?
"You're stupid."	This is a real self-esteem builder.
"Listen to your elders, they know more than you."	What happens when the elder is a priest who rapes you, or an unethical boss?
"People who don't have a lot of money are lazy."	Some of the entry-level workers on my job sites work harder than most people I know. Unfortunately, most of them haven't had great educations in finance.
"Why can't you be more like your sister?"	How about if I'm more like me?

INFLICTING GUILT ON YOURSELF

Sometimes you inflict the pain on yourself, feeling guilt about something you did. You spend months and years reliving it in your mind, wondering what it would be like if the outcome were different. *What if I made that real estate investment? I would have so much more money now! What if I forgave my mother before she died? What if I didn't leave that person? I wouldn't be alone and sad now.*

TAKING A PERSONAL INVENTORY AND GETTING READY TO MOVE FORWARD

Take a few minutes, put the book down, and reflect on your emotional DNA. What emotions are affecting your life negatively and getting your Relationship Quadrant out of balance? Can you pinpoint an event, a person, or a specific time in your life that triggered these feelings?

When we allow past painful experiences to become our emotional DNA, we create deep psychological and physical pains such as loneliness, depression, inability to express our true feelings, and fatigue, all of which jeopardize our well-being. Past events, failures, and regrets burden our capacity for present happiness, sustaining the belief that we are unable to succeed. Helplessness sets in when the focus is on our faults.

Instead of repeating and living in the past, it's time to write a brand-new story. The future is full of possibility, and it is unwritten. If you are suffering from pain rooted in the past, it's time to realize something: *You are not your past.* No matter what happened in the past, you can focus on what you want to be, rather than what happened to you. It's time to put the past in the past.

That thing that happened is over. What is it that you want to accomplish now? How do you want to live, now that you know you can't stay in a place of blame and shame any longer? You can start by accepting the responsibility for how you are going to feel and how you are going to act. The pain you felt from someone or something can stop if you just decide it will. Unless you allow it, this event or person is no longer a part of your life. It is not able to harm you anymore. If you have trouble adopting this attitude or figuring out how you can approach it, therapy and/or support groups may be a good place to start. Still, *you* have to be the one to take that first step toward changing your perspective and moving forward.

At some point you have to face the fact that you are the one making the decision to stay in this painful place. You're doing it to yourself. Ask yourself: why are you allowing it to continue? Why does it feel comfortable for you to be in pain? Do you understand that you have the strength to break away from these memories?

MY ELEPHANT REVELATION

When I was in the mountains of Thailand, I saw 6,000-pound elephants with ropes around their legs tied to two-inch-thick wooden pegs that were hammered into the ground. Forced to give rides to entire families seated on heavy metal benches on their backs, these animals went without breaks for ten hours in a row, day after day. It was heartbreaking to witness these majestic animals being treated this way. With just a tiny bit of effort, the enormous elephants could have pulled the pegs out of the ground and run to freedom in the jungle.

As I drove past this scene on my way to the visit the elephants at the sanctuary (where people don't ride them), I asked the guide why they didn't run away. He said they were tied with the same type of rope when they were babies. They tried to get loose then, but the ropes held them. As the years went on and the elephants grew stronger than the ropes, they still believed those ropes could hold them.

You're not a baby elephant anymore. You're an enormously powerful being who can break free anytime you choose.

YOU ARE IN CONTROL

Realize that you can take control of your life because you're an adult with free will. Give yourself permission to let go of the damaged DNA from your past and to bury the excuses and stories about why you can't succeed. Now is the time to reshape your life.

How do you make that happen? It takes a conscious effort to recognize when those old feelings arise from old patterns. When you're aware, you're able to make the decision to let them go. You choose what you think, so choose to focus on the opposite of the negative thoughts. Focusing on something positive immediately changes the way you feel.

Surround yourself with positive people who treat you with respect, generosity, and love. Select friends and family members who build you up and help you to see the best things about yourself. Equally important, these people will tell you the truth in a constructive way—they don't denigrate you or make you feel "less than." Place yourself in activities and environments with people who are living lives that you admire.

Release the people who trigger bad feelings, even if they are family and you feel guilty about doing it. Cut out people and situations that constantly take from you, breaking you down and draining your vitality. This is your life, and it's your responsibility to make it the best one you can.

People tell you to forgive and forget. Feel free to do both or neither, while steering yourself far from the negative things that happened to you. You are not obligated to forgive anyone, unless you want to and it helps you to heal. Some things are unforgivable. It's perfectly fine to walk away without the forgiveness and without the anger. Move away from negativity and into a space where you treat yourself and others with kindness, respect, and positivity.

Use Your Experiences to Create a Better You

When you commit to a present that is free from the contamination of your painful past, it doesn't mean you pretend the past never happened. Your history is real, but it's not who you are and it's not how you have to be. You went through it—why not gain from it?

What can you use from your traumatic experience? Is it possible that the same experience you're viewing as a roadblock to happiness could be something that creates a positive dimension of your personality? Could you actually spin this "defect" into an attribute that helps you succeed?

There's a saying among soldiers: "What doesn't kill you makes you stronger, and if it kills you, it makes your mother stronger." If you were beaten, can it make you gentler? If you experienced a lack of money or food, can you now empathize with others who face the same plight? Can being bullied encourage you treat others with acceptance? My answer to all three is YES.

Running from your past is exhausting. Instead, embrace what happened. Reflect back on your experience. Pull something positive from it and use it to your advantage.

LEARNING FROM THE SON OF A TERRORIST

I recommend watching a TED talk by Zak Ebrahim, titled "I am the son of a terrorist." Translated into forty-one languages with over two million views, it's one of the most heartfelt stories I've ever heard.

This man was seven years old when his father helped plan the 1993 World Trade Center bombing. He grew up in an environment of hate and shame. The father's nefarious dealings required the family to move twenty times before Zak turned nineteen.

Zak's frequent moves and chubby physique didn't help him make friends, and he was bullied at each new school. He spent a lot of time alone watching TV and credits Jewish talk show host Jon Stewart with being the father who influenced him to accept others. This is especially ironic, because his biological father taught him to hate Jews.

He now spends his life teaching others about tolerance, respect, and love. He exemplifies how to release a toxic influence, as he cut ties with his father. He shows how the events that tormented his youth, being the target of violence, became the primary reason he was able to learn to judge others by individual experience and treat people with kindness. If the son of a terrorist can move forward, you can too.

I love this example because it shows that even if you had inadequate role models, you're not doomed. You can find inspiration all around you, even from someone you will never meet.

CRAFTING MY NEW NARRATIVE

At twenty-one, I came to the realization that it was time to accept responsibility for my life and stop blaming others for the sadness and anger that I felt because of the abuse and neglect I suffered as a child. It took many more years to begin to trust people and gain control of the explosive temper I inherited from my mother.

I held on to the pain for far too long, believing that it gave me an edge. I mistakenly thought that if I let go of my aggressive nature and the need to always be right, I wouldn't succeed. I'd lose my edge in business.

But I was tired of being unhappy and was ready for the hole in my heart to heal. I chose to focus on patience and gratitude for the things I have instead of looking backward. When I was lonely, I took action and surrounded myself with the right kind of people and put myself in environments that were conducive to positive growth.

When I feel despair or negativity, I talk to someone who cares about me. The simple act of thinking about something I love instead of something that I hate puts a smile on my face. Doing these things has given me the security and freedom to make better choices.

I still lose my temper occasionally, but I bounce back fast and I have learned how to forgive myself when I fall down for a minute. When you allow yourself to be distanced from your past, you gain a new perspective, create a healthy emotional DNA, and propel yourself into a life that you feel ecstatic about living.

Friends are like fudge,
mostly sweet
with a couple of nuts

CHAPTER 2

Family and Friendships

For human beings, the need for connection with others is the strongest force in the Universe. Some might argue that procreation is a more powerful drive, but sex is just another form of connection. What about food and self-preservation? A parent would go hungry if that meant they could feed their starving child. You might even put your life on the line to save someone you love.

To be whole, it is imperative to form and maintain healthy bonds and loving relationships with people or animals. When you lack meaningful connections or you engage in frequent conflict with others, your Relationship Quadrant is out of equilibrium. To find balance in your life, your relationships have to function properly, providing support and love.

Knowing what constitutes a good relationship can be challenging, especially when studies show that 85 percent of families are dysfunctional. Boundaries of what's expected and acceptable aren't always defined, leaving plenty of opportunity for misunderstandings and hurt feelings. As with so many things in life, you get out what you put in. If you make the investment of time and attention, you will be rewarded with the ability to give and receive a special, deep, and unconditional love. What's better than that?

NURTURING FAMILY RELATIONSHIPS

If you're feeling disconnected and lonely, try spending more time on the original social network, your family. One of the biggest problems with the way we live today is that physical and emotional separation from our families has become normal. Children are bred to get good grades and go off to college, many times in a different city or state. Then children become adults who start separate lives in cities far from their families, growing distant from the people who love them the most.

When life gets busy with building careers, forming new networks, and raising families, connections with family can become weaker and weaker. Months or even years go by without talking to the people who were once closest to us. It's no surprise that so many people feel isolated and alone.

Why do we do this? It doesn't make any emotional sense. Humans are pack animals and we thrive when we a part of a family, even if that family isn't related by blood. Evidence of this basic need for family is seen in the momentum of co-living developments that share communal spaces and responsibilities, where complete strangers become a family unit.

We can make it on our own, but it's so much easier and more satisfying with a built-in support system. My family is spread out all over the country. My husband's family is on the other side of the world. When my daughter was born, we were completely on our own, overwhelmed and exhausted. There was no one there to make a meal or watch the baby for an hour while we got some rest.

We struggled alone in a situation where we had no experience and made the best of it. Thank goodness for books on what to expect! It wasn't that our family didn't care about us, but there was little they could do, being thousands of miles away and having to tend to their own careers and families.

Years later my goddaughter's first child was born. Understanding the importance of a family's help in those first few weeks, we flew across the country to offer our support. The scenario was entirely different than ours.

The house was bustling with family members. My goddaughter and her husband chose to live in the same neighborhood where they grew up. Both sets of parents and grandparents live only a few miles away and were more than happy to pitch in and offer all that was needed, and lots of love.

The entire flight home I couldn't stop thinking about why people would intentionally isolate themselves from family. What could be more important than these connections? Whether you're miles away, down the street, or under the same roof, make the decision to strengthen these ties. Do everything you can to keep the bonds of family intact.

We share an irreplaceable kinship with parents, siblings, aunts and uncles, grandparents, and cousins that grew up with us. Who else can understand the inner workings of your family? Who else has witnessed the transformation of the person you have become today? Treat them as the priceless assets in your life that they are.

If you have close relationships with these people, consider yourself blessed. If you've grown apart, take steps to come back together. Be proactive: write a letter, send a text, make a call, and set up a date to begin making new memories together.

TOXIC RELATIVES

You get what you get with family, and unfortunately sometimes a close relative is toxic. Unlike a bad friend, deciding to cut ties with a family member is more complex because of your familial loyalty and other family members' relationships to that person. Perhaps you've given multiple concessions and really tried to forgive someone, but they are incapable of changing. The transgressions they commit against you repeat without fail.

In this case it is completely acceptable to remove yourself from a person who perpetuates your suffering. When you make that decision, you also need to let go of the hatred and anger inside of you. Realize that other members of your family may not share your feelings. They may still want to be connected to that person. That's their journey and it's OK. There's no reason to jeopardize relationships with other family members over your decision.

HOW TO PARENT

If you are raising children, you may have wondered if you're a good enough parent. Are you repeating patterns, doing what was done to you just because it was your experience? If you recall that these things felt bad or wrong when you were a kid, here's your opportunity break that cycle for good. Stop doing those things.

If you make a mistake, apologize to your kid. It feels a little weird to admit to a child that you don't know what the heck you're doing sometimes and that you made a mistake. But trust me, they appreciate it, and by apologizing, you could prevent damage to their emotional DNA.

Set up behavioral expectations when kids are toddlers and follow through until they become adults. Disciplined kids and pets are happier and better behaved when they know the boundaries and what is expected of them.

When your kids eventually become teenagers with raging hormones, they will be able to keep their bad attitudes in check because they learned that respect for their parents is nonnegotiable. The bonus here is that they won't become icky adults either. Go back to the elephant story in the last chapter; it applies here too. The lessons you learn when you're young are ingrained in you for life.

Our house is not kid-centric—as much as we love our daughter, our lives are about our entire family—everything doesn't revolve around her needs. However, if we make a commitment to her, we're going to move mountains to try to keep it. Show your children what trust and follow-through looks like so they can do it and will expect it in their relationships.

Nothing Is as Important as Your Time

Don't give your social media and news feeds priority over your kids. Being on your phone all the time, paying attention to other people's lives, is stealing from your kids and yourself (plus the phone radiation is pretty bad for you).

If you're busy with life, make an appointment with your kid at least once a week to do something that nourishes your souls. Play guitar together, throw a ball, build a snowman, take the dog for a walk together, play a board game, cook pancakes, draw smiley faces. Be that parent. If you ever feel like you don't have the time, listen to the Harry Chapin song "Cat's in the Cradle." It's a song about a guy who never has time for his kid. The kid grows up and the dad retires. Now the dad wants to spend some time and the kid is too busy for his dad. It's tragic and totally avoidable.

Allow Your Child to Be a Child

Don't force your kids to be little molds of you. I know you want them to have every opportunity and all the advantages they can, but let them be kids first. It's fair to expect that they try to successfully complete the things they start. But you have to realize that all kids are not the same—some have problems, disabilities, idiosyncrasies, and unique talents.

Worrying about things like what college they will get into when they are in the fifth grade is obsessive and premature. Behaving this way stresses them out at a time in their life when they should be carefree. Love them for who they are and give them the support they need to grow into productive, decent people.

The future is going to be a radically different place. Very few of us know what it will entail. Things you consider important now may not matter in ten years. Take it easy on your kids and yourself. If you raise them right, one day they will become your very best friends.

FRIENDSHIPS

You can't choose your family, but you can pick your friends. Motivational speaker Wayne Dyer said, "Friends are God's apology for your family." Friendship is a precious opportunity to select the exact type of person who can make your life complete. It's like casting the actors for your very own movie.

Have you always wanted a funny big sister who knows exactly how to cheer you up? She's out there. What about a friend to share your love of wine? He's out there. They're all out there, because friends come in every age, gender, race, and cultural background.

If you have a small family and holiday celebrations were underwhelming, your friend might come from a large family who invites you to their festive celebrations. I have a Moroccan friend just like this. She invents reasons to have huge gatherings in her home, like Love Day, where we eat delicious food and dance to live drum circles in her living room. When she invited a group of twelve friends to join her family on a journey to Marrakesh, we made memories that are as rich as anything I've ever experienced.

Friends can be the mentors who inspire us to move ahead in our careers, be better parents, or learn how to connect with our community. Wise older friends, with years of knowledge, can show us how to be more patient and avoid the pitfalls they've already encountered. Younger friends are in tune with what's going on in the worlds of music, fashion, and technology. They keep us hip and engage our brains.

Friendships Worth Having

How do we build valuable friendships like these? There has to be positivity, lifting each other up, and highlighting the good in the other person. There's something that you like about each other, something that is appealing, even fascinating, something that compels you to want to spend time together.

Then you must actually spend time together sharing experiences on a regular basis, even if it's just by email or phone. It's this time that is invested that creates the memories that form the bonds of your friendship. You can't create strong relationships if you don't give them attention.

After you invest the time, trust is built. You are able to be vulnerable, sharing core parts of who you are and what you want. For a friendship to be meaningful, you have to be able to depend on that person even when it is inconvenient for them.

I remember a very funny scene from Larry David's show *Curb Your Enthusiasm*. He's walking down the street and bumps into a "friend." The friend tells him about something terrible that happened, and Larry asks him if he need any help. The friend accepts Larry's offer, only to be told by Larry that he didn't really mean it and that was just something people say.

To have a friend, you've got to be a friend. There's no way around this. Euripides said, "One loyal friend is better than 10,000 relatives." On the other hand, if you have a friend who is never there for you, never spends time with you or shares her or his life with you, it's probably time to look for a better friend.

If you're unsure of where or how to make good friends, volunteer in an activity that interests you. If you love animals, work with a pet adoption group. If you love the ocean, get involved with a beach cleanup group. People who volunteer are helpful and outgoing. These are exactly the types of people you want as friends.

WHEN CONFLICTS ARISE

Don't let arguments stand in the way of maintaining good relationships.

When you've developed a close connection with another person, you've earned trust. Trust allows you expose yourself to someone else without fear of rejection.

Ever since we were little, we were taught to not make mistakes because getting something wrong means there's something wrong with us. We approach disagreements or misunderstandings with an internal sense of having to show we are right.

However, attachment to being right only perpetuates struggle. Whenever I'm fighting with more than one person at a time, I step back and look at the common denominator, me. It's not likely that all these other people are wrong and I'm innocent. I've come to a point where I am more interested in finding a resolution than in being right.

Trusting my friends and family to give me feedback on my behavior helps me to gain perspective on how to change my attitude or actions and stop conflict. Learning how to say "I'm wrong, I understand, and I'm sorry" empowers you. Reducing conflict reduces stress, which makes me happier and allows me to sustain relationships with people I love and people who love me.

One final thought is that lonely and depressed people are more likely get sick and die prematurely because they're prone to overeat, smoke, drink, do drugs, and work too hard. Recommit to family and seek out meaningful friendships to form life-affirming connections. You never need to be lonely when you can experience the brilliant balance that comes from sharing your life with others.

The best and
most beautiful things
in this world
cannot be seen
or even heard,
but must be
felt with the heart.

- Anne Sullivan
(Helen Keller's Teacher)

CHAPTER 3

Romantic Relationships

The last chapter illustrated the importance of having healthy connections with others. In our society, romantic relationships fill a similar need of bonding with another, but include the added value of intimacy that is shared between two people.

These private, intense connections, where you yearn for physical contact, are nature's way of making us "couple up." Desire for another person can be overwhelming, sometimes uncontrollable, and can leave us powerless to make rational decisions. The same area of our brain that controls addiction also controls how we feel when we are in love. The result of all these chemicals igniting in our brain is that our biology temporarily takes over our decision-making abilities.

FALLING IN LOVE

When the heart wants what it wants, all sense of reason goes out of the window. In the beginning, a partner becomes a priority over everything else in our lives. We've all seen people abandon decades-old relationships because the person they fall in love with doesn't like their family or friends.

Your romantic relationships could be the most impactful parts of your life. Do they empower you to be your best self, making your life richer, or do they diminish your experiences—within and outside of the relationship?

Your lover is the family you choose, your very best friend, and likely the most important relationship in your life. In order to bloom, it's critical that you gain the awareness of how to repel the wrong partners, attract the right person, and then cultivate a balanced relationship with your significant other.

FINDING THE RIGHT PARTNER

There's a lid for every pot. With almost eight billion people on our planet, more than one person out there is the right fit for you. Once you begin to see love in yourself, you will attract others who love you.

Self-esteem and self-worth are attracting qualities. Solid people want to be with partners who have something to offer in return. Think about what you have to offer.

Healthy relationships are built when you have gifts to share. Gifts are compassion, a sense of humor, honesty, positivity, loyalty, generosity, and pieces of your personality that complement a potential partner.

Need is not a gift. If you're coming from a place of needing someone else to fix you, or pay for your lifestyle, or solve your problems, you'll end up attracting a person who wants to be in a relationship with someone who is broken. It's a great recipe for a toxic union.

Nonnegotiables in a Partner

You're reading a book about how to balance all of the quadrants in your life. Clearly you are interested in being a whole person, which makes you a very desirable partner. Now you get to decide what you want, and you start by understanding what is important to you in a mate.

You should never settle, but you do have to be reasonable. What are your nonnegotiables? An arbitrary list of things like how much money someone makes, how old they are, or what they look like should take a back seat to a list of how this person make you feel, if they are honest, and if you can imagine building a life with them.

Physical traits or monetary status are fleeting and not foundations of how to select the right life partner. You must define the things that really matter to you, the areas where you will not compromise.

For instance, if marriage and kids are important to you, your potential mate must want them as well. Maybe they don't know if you are the person they want to marry in the very beginning, but they know that having a family is a life goal that they want to accomplish.

Are your beliefs and ethics in sync? Are you deeply religious and do you expect a partner to practice prayer the way you do? Is having a pet an essential part of your life? Are your monetary goals in line with each other?

The nonnegotiable list should be relatively small because it's OK to be flexible on traits that aren't fundamental in your life. Yet the older people get, the more rigid they become about what they will accept in a partner. They expect others to eat the exact same way, or to hold identical political opinions, or to have all the same interests.

In truth, having these differences between partners could create the most exciting and interesting life you can imagine. Do yourself a favor. Open your mind to the possibility that what you think you want may never show up, but what you really need is all around you.

My Mr. Right

Before I met my husband, I hoped that I would marry someone ten years older who was experienced and wealthy. When Mr. Right arrived, he was ten years younger than me, just getting started in life, and had about $200 to his name.

He liked cars and guns, which I couldn't care less about. Yoga and massages were more my jam, two things in which he still has no interest. Yet here was this guy who was my intellectual equal, the greatest lover, my emotional companion, a man who was solid as a rock, who I could trust, and who wanted the same things in life that I did.

I embraced the idea that we could build a life together that would last forever. Sometimes you need to abandon ideas about things that don't really matter and hit home runs with the curve balls life throws you. I'm madly in love with my husband. I go to bed every night and wake every morning feeling grateful that he is mine. We've been together for thirteen years and every day it gets better.

REPEATING PATTERNS THAT DON'T WORK

If you are in a pattern of selecting lovers who are wrong for you, it's time to start seeing the red flags before you invest a lot of time in a relationship that will ultimately fail. If you find yourself repeatedly going out with a certain type that isn't working for you, examine what you are attracting and change it.

Your goal is to become wise enough to stay away or brave enough to walk away from these relationships. The first time you get swept off your feet and blindsided, you're innocent. We all learn from making mistakes. But if you continue making this a habit, doing the same wrong thing over and over, it's your fault.

When you understand that you possess the ability to make better decisions, you will start selecting appropriate partners. Many years ago I read a poem by Portia Nelson that changed my dating life. In her poem, a girl walks down the street and falls in a hole.

She's helpless, feels like it's not her fault, and takes forever to get out. Later she walks down the same street, pretends she doesn't see the hole, and falls in again. She is shocked that she fell in the hole again, but won't take responsibility and takes a long time to get out.

She walks down that same street again and falls back into the hole because it's a habit. This time she knows that she is to blame and gets out of the hole right away. The next day she walks down the same street, sees the hole, and walks around it. From then on, when she takes a walk, she goes down another street.

It's really that simple. Stop falling in the same hole and go down another street. On that new street, keep your eyes open for holes. Don't fall in them—or, better yet, change streets again. I put that poem up on my wall. I looked at it every day and eventually I stopped falling in holes.

PAY ATTENTION TO RED FLAGS

When you're dating someone, do you ever get a glimpse of something about his or her core behavior that you really don't like? Pay attention to that feeling. Does this person treat you exceptionally well, but always talk about how horrible their last partner was and how everything was their fault? The ex they're incessantly badmouthing will become you one day.

Does this person treat strangers, wait staff, or others poorly when they don't get their way? Does it make you cringe, but you think there's no way they could ever treat you that way? They will. They are showing you who they really are.

With those rose-colored love glasses you're wearing, you see what you hope for instead of what is real. When love has made you blind, it's time to bring in family and friends to judge for you. What do the people who care about you think? Listen to them and listen to your gut. There's always another bus coming down the road. Look at the signs next time and get on the right one.

REJECTION IS PROTECTION

When someone doesn't love you back, that's wonderful. You can be 100 percent certain that they're not the right person for you. No matter how great this person looks on paper, it would not have worked out.

Rejection is the Universe's way of protecting you. When you look at it that way, you will realize it's ridiculous to continue loving someone who doesn't love you back. It's still hard when your emotions go haywire and the loss of that love is real to you.

Give yourself a week to grieve, cry it out, and begin to be emotionally available for the right person. Tell yourself that you have worth and the right person is around the next corner. Even if you don't yet believe it, repeat those words to yourself in front of a mirror many times a day.

You also need to stay away from people who are emotionally unavailable to you. They act like they're interested so you will feed their ego, but they never make substantial time for you. They text you and string you along, but they never commit or give you real love. This is rejection veiled as attention. You deserve more than that. Move on.

The beginning of a relationship should feel easy and smooth. If you're pulling teeth to get someone to be with you, it's one of those red flags you need to see. If you're the one who is leading someone else on, stop it. You can't meet the right person when you're hanging on to the wrong person.

CHANGING PEOPLE

It should go without saying, but I will list the nonnegotiables of dating in the event that you're still confused. If your potential partner is an addict, is a liar, is unreliable, is dating or married to someone else, is unkind, is noncommittal, makes you feel uncomfortable or sad, degrades you, is in massive debt, or is a criminal—run the other way. Don't try to change people.

Robert Heinlein said it best: "Never attempt to teach a pig to sing; it wastes your time and annoys the pig." Have the courage to be yourself, to show another person who you really are. More importantly, believe it when someone shows you who they are.

Don't fall in love with someone's potential to be something else.

If you're unhappy or lonely in a new relationship or it's just plain obvious that it's not working for you, have the confidence to leave and find one that does. If you're thinking that the person will be different and hoping you can make their lid fit your pot, stop. You don't need to make it fit, because there are literally billions of other lids out there, some that already fit perfectly. Save your energy for those people.

WHEN YOU'VE FOUND THE RIGHT ONE

Listen and be flexible. I've said it before: it's better to be happy than right, especially with your romantic partner. Listening to your partner with a caring, kind, and open mind is the most important skill that you need to succeed in a relationship.

Hear what your partner is saying and be willing to do the things that will make you both happy. When you want different things, find a way to agree to do whatever it is that makes both people feel like they have value.

It's not about persuading the other person to do what you want. You have to want to find real meaning in what the other person is expressing. Pick your battles. If it's truly important, stand your ground, and if it really isn't, then it's OK to give in.

Sharing the Power

Be flexible and share the power. You're with this person because you like what they have to offer. You trust them, and their judgment matters to you. They're your best friend, the person you turn to for advice.

Couples who share the power do better together over the long run. There is less space for resentment because they made the decisions together. Whether it's life changing, like a job or a move, or less impactful, like where to go on vacation or what kind of car to buy, make these decisions together and empower each other.

The Importance of Being True

Love unconditionally and be willing to receive in return. Expose yourself to the bone, be vulnerable, reveal your flaws, and allow your partner to do the same. Be true to your partner and yourself.

Don't lie. Lying to someone who counts on you is being selfish, like a child who wants to get his or her way regardless of the consequences. People lie when they feel their partner is being unreasonable or they know what they want is wrong. Have the courage to get it out in the open, stand up for what you want—or don't do it.

You must be dependable. If you say you're going to do something, no matter how small, then do it. Every time you fail to be reliable, the mutual respect and trust that took years to create is compromised. Knowing that someone has your back and you have theirs is priceless. It makes a person feel protected when they know the other person is always going to be there for them, just as the sun comes up each day.

HOW TO FIGHT

When you disagree, do it without tearing the other person down. Try to focus on what you love about the other person and let them know. It took many years to learn that when I told my husband, "You are better than this, I believe you are a winner"—rather than "You are wrong and stupid for doing this"—he wanted to rise to the challenge and do the right thing.

It takes one person to stop a fight, because it's almost impossible to fight with someone who won't fight back.

It's common to hurt the ones we love, acting in ways that would be embarrassing if other people saw. We do this because we know they will forgive us. But that is backward thinking, because these are the people who deserve our best. When you catch yourself being ruthless, calm down, apologize, and start over by behaving the way you want to be treated. When you screw up, ask for forgiveness and change that behavior.

SAYING GOODBYE

Even though you have invested a lot of time and energy into making something work, sometimes it just doesn't. Maybe you started off with the wrong partner in the first place and just kept trying to make it work so you wouldn't fail. Or maybe you're afraid to leave because you'll lose money, status, or companionship.

It's OK to move on when it's not right, when it clearly should be over. Cut your losses and look forward to finding the right person. Don't tiptoe into another pool and cheat.

Don't beg for someone to stay when they want to go. Don't get pregnant to solve your problems. That only drags children into your doomed relationship. Practice nonattachment and learn from every goodbye. Hearts break, and hearts mend. Being in an ill-fitted relationship is like wearing clothes that itch; you might look good to everyone else, but you never feel right.

loyal
honest
affectionate
dependable
present
chemistry
kind
home

He is happiest,

be he king or peasant,

who finds peace in his home.

- Johann Wolfgang von Goethe

CHAPTER 4

Home

Our home is the physical place that contrasts with all others. It's where we leave the external, outside world to enter the internal, a space within. It's the place where we feel safe, where we recharge, a haven from the rest of the world.

Home is the sanctuary where we have control. This is the place where our mask comes off, our hair is messy, we can pick our nose, we put on the comfy sweats with holes in them. We no longer have to make polite conversation, censor our speech, or be "on."

THE IDEA OF HOME

The "spatial" relationship we have with the place we inhabit should offer us comfort, peace, and security and should provide an environment where we can be our true selves. Do you take full advantage of this space for your emotional and physical shelter from the outside world? Is your home providing security or stress?

Learning how to maximize the benefits of this interaction with our private spaces helps us to create harmony in our

Relationships Quadrant. (If privacy is high on the list of what you value at home, be aware that devices like Alexa and Echo listen to everything you say.)

Do you plant deep roots, staying in one place for a lifetime? Are you more of a rolling stone, content with moving to a new place every few years? Or do you feel most comfortable living as a digital nomad, traveling the world one Airbnb at time?

Is your home palatial, a 250-square-foot studio, or an RV out in nature? The ideal of home is no longer only about the physical building—instead it's the space behind closed doors, where you're the boss and you make the laws. It might be the only place in the world where you exert total control over your environment. You decide the temperature, what type of music is playing, the smells, the level of activity, and what it looks like.

THE TRUTH ABOUT PRETTY ROOMS

Having spent the last two decades as a professional interior designer, I have seen the impact that homes have on people's lives. Where and how you live are an expression of your authentic self, often a mirror of who you really are. If you're feeling inadequate because your home doesn't look like those on your social feeds, magazines, or the "afters" on TV, stop.

Before we shoot and film these rooms, we spend hours cleaning them, hiding all the cords, placing accessories in absurd configurations that no normal person would ever use, and then lighting them perfectly. It's similar to photoshopped models who actually have pimples and cellulite that we never see.

The feeling of home doesn't come by hiring an interior designer or purchasing fancy things. It's what's under the hood that makes it a home. However, having a space that you feel proud of and want to share with others does facilitate an environment for better relationships with self or friends and family. When you feel good about your home, you enjoy it and want to share it with others.

ORGANIZATION

We all have different level of what we expect and what we can tolerate when it comes to being organized. Minimalist, maximalist, or somewhere in between, the items in your home should be things you love or things you use, and you should be able to find all of them with ease.

If you're hanging on to a bunch of crap that you have no emotional attachment to or that has no utility, ask yourself why. It creates stress and wastes time to look for things you can't find, digging through closets and drawers that are packed to maximum capacity. It can also be a waste of money when you wind up purchasing the same things you already have, because they were hidden in the clutter.

I'm a big fan of *Tidying Up with Marie Kondo* on Netflix. If you know you need to get organized, watch a few episodes for inspiration. Clutter equals chaos, so clear it out. Don't allocate space for anything broken in your life. Fix these items or remove them from your home.

COMFORT

Enjoying your home means being able to relax: not only mentally, but physically. Bringing comfort into your space is a matter of paying attention to the details in the areas you use. It's also diverting resources to install the furnishings that make the spaces work for you.

Sleeping on a mattress and using pillows that properly support your body and neck means the difference between waking up feeling refreshed or enduring neck and back pain on a daily basis. If you have to make tough budget choices, spend money on your bed and bedding. Getting a good night of sleep is the foundation for a successful next day.

Create comfort in spaces that matter to you like a place to chill, watch TV, or read a book. If you love to cook, outfit your kitchen with the proper pots, pans, and utensils to prepare delicious meals. Make your bathroom a mini spa, with plush towels, candles, soaking salts, and other pampering products. If there's a place or thing in your home that makes you uncomfortable, take care of it.

FUNCTIONALITY

Every area in your home should have a function. Pay attention to rooms or spaces that are wasted opportunities. Are you paying to heat and cool areas you never use, and at the same time complaining that you don't have enough space?

A cost-effective way to work with what you already have, but make it all work better, is to hire a stager for a few days. They come to your house and "shop at home." A professional gives your old things new life by simply moving the existing furniture and accessories around so the spaces function properly.

A professional stager, or a friend with "the organization gene," can also help you get organized and weed out things that need to go. Using your space in its most effective layout is like a tune-up for your home. Rearranging your space creates a new perspective, physically and emotionally.

Have your space needs changed? Has the need for an office space for your business superseded the need for a formal dining room? Do you have a guest room filled with junk that you don't need, but wish you had space to meditate or work out? Does anyone ever go into your living room? Would it be more functional to create an arts and crafts space in that area?

Many very successful people employ principles of feng shui, the Chinese art of creating harmonious surroundings to enhance balance, in their home. They believe that it has an impact on their happiness, health, and wealth. I find that many of the principles are common sense and do actually make you feel better.

It all circles back to the functionality and arrangement of your home. For instance, if you work facing the entry to a room, you will likely feel more secure than having your back to the door and being caught off guard when someone unexpected enters. Check out a YouTube video or read a book about feng shui, and borrow whatever works for you.

SHOW OFF WHO YOU ARE

Is your home a reflection of who you are and your values? Do you have a sense of pride when you invite guests in? If interior design and aesthetics are important to you, then feather your nest. Don't make excuses like "I don't have the money."

Sell things you don't love and discover Freecycle, yard sales, and thrift shops. I have heard so many people say, "I'll wait until my kids are grown to make my home nice." It's your house and your rules. Pets and kids follow your lead. I have both. I set boundaries. I have a well-designed home.

You might think you don't have any design ability. You can find everything you need to know about how to put things together on Pinterest and Instagram. Imitate what's happening in those rooms.

Start moving things around in your space to make it resemble the rooms you love. Make it your own by displaying your collections and painting the walls your favorite colors, or using removable wallpaper if you can't paint. Don't sit around wishing you that you could live in your dream house—build it!

WORKING FROM HOME

Millions of people now work from home. With the gig economy, that number will continue to grow. There are many benefits to doing this, including saving money and time on a commute.

The number-one rule for working at home is separation of space. When work is over, you have to be able to leave the "office" and start being at home. If you have an entirely segregated space, this is easy. When you're finished working, you leave the space.

However, if the same space is doing double duty, you must carve out an area that is dedicated only to work. It could be a cabinet, or a closet with a desk inside, where curtains or sliding doors can close at the end of work time. Using a standing screen in front of your workspace is great solution to hide "the office." The simple act of placing an attractive cloth over a desk filled with work product also solves the issue.

Working from home is a wonderful way to have complete control over your work environment, the way it looks, feels, and sounds. You just need to "leave work at work" in order to create a balanced and healthy home atmosphere. Being healthy at work is important too—I recommend a standing desk so you can avoid sitting the entire day.

SHARING YOUR SPACE

If you don't like being alone, you never need to be. You can share your space with family, a pet, roommates, travelers, or even move into a co-living setup. Even if you live alone in a tiny space, you can invite others in for coffee or a full-blown meal.

Search YouTube for videos on topics such as "How New Yorkers entertain in a small space." You'll see how even the smallest of apartments can function for a gathering.

My family is very busy during the week with work, exercise classes, continuing education, and after-school activities, leaving little time to visit with friends. But come the weekend, we get social. Friday is an open-door policy at our house. There are always a few extra servings of dinner for unexpected guests.

We installed a disco ball on the ceiling of our living room, transforming our home into a personal karaoke dance club. If no one shows up, we still dance and have leftovers for lunch on Saturday. Enjoy your space by inviting people to celebrate it with you.

NATURE AS NURTURE

Most of us live in cities; we're inside all day and we have limited connection with nature. On the days when you're inside, open the curtains and let the sunlight in. Houseplants bring the outdoors in and they also clean the air.

If you'd like to get more oxygen and clean air in your bedroom at night, place a snake plant in your bedroom. At night this plant absorbs the carbon monoxide that you exhale and releases oxygen. Snake plants are hearty and don't require much attention.

Even if you don't cook, having fresh herbs like rosemary, basil, and mint plants in your kitchen is a wonderful way to connect with nature. You can also use the leaves in water for a spa feeling, or just to make plain water more appealing. Fresh mint tea, made by pouring boiling water over the mint leaves and served hot or cold, is divine.

THE NEW NOMAD

All of these principles apply to modern nomads, who bounce from place to place. With the massive inventory of Airbnb spaces, it's incredibly cool to be able to live in well-designed places that suit your personal style and meet your needs. You have all the benefits of home without being attached to a specific location, a lease agreement, or a mortgage.

You still exert control over your environment and make the rules when you enter the door, but you get to experience different locales and cultures and meet people all over the world. The nomad illustrates how the idea of home is really what is in your heart and being in a space where you feel comfortable. If you are a nomad and you miss that feeling of leaving your own mark on a physical space, travel with a significant item like a framed picture, a coffee mug, or a candle with a certain smell. It will help to transform each new setting into "your home."

These ideas are widely held concepts of what makes a space feel like home. The beauty of home is that it is whatever you want it to be, your own unique space. If it makes you happy to live in a mess of paper, surfaces thick with dust, never opening the curtains, the go for it. If you walk in from a long day and say, "Ahhh, this is heaven," then keep it dark and dirty. This is home for you, and you are the ruler of this kingdom.

WHEN HOME DOESN'T FEEL HOMEY

If you're not feeling a sense of comfort and peace in your home, ask yourself why. Is it the people sharing your space? Do you need to find new roommates or partners?

Is the location too dark, too noisy, to confining? Is it run-down or embarrassing? Does the location feel unsafe? Is it too expensive, forcing you to stay at a job you hate, or live with people who you don't want in your personal space to help pay the bills?

Are there necessary home improvement projects that are never started or never finished? Do you notice stains in the carpet or on or the sofa that depress you, but you never take the time to clean them? Do the piles of papers, the stuffed junk drawers, the disorganized cabinets, the peeling paint, the loads of garbage in your garage, or your unruly garden upset you? Then you need to address them.

There's no need to stay in a place that doesn't work. Move or fix the issues, whether they are material or human. Live only with people who are contributing to your happiness. Don't allow the only environment you have control over to take control of you. Do not be a passive participant in your own ecosystem.

Take action to ensure that the space you call home is truly a place of serenity and security, not a source of turmoil and fear. Create an oasis separate from the external world. When you do this, you take a crucial step toward attaining balance in your Relationships Quadrant.

PART II
FINANCES

To attract
money,
you must focus
on wealth.

- Rhonda Byrne

CHAPTER 5

Finances

It's true that money can't buy you happiness, but it's awfully hard to be happy without it. As children we spend years in school learning about history, writing skills, science, and math but almost no attention is given to personal finances: how to make, invest, and manage money.

Finance often feels like a foreign language to too many people. For most people, the mastery of money, intimidating and complex, is the scariest of all four quadrants. Because money plays such an important role in our lives, being out of balance in the Finances Quadrant can create perceived and real events that negatively impact our relationships, wellness, and spirituality. Like compounded interest, the problems grow bigger and more stressful. But it doesn't have to be this way.

Gaining financial literacy by educating yourself is how you can control your financial life. Financial literacy occurs when you understand basic facts about money and personal finances. Your financial IQ expands when you develop the skills to achieve your financial goals. When you become financially literate and increase your financial IQ, you gain the confidence and ability to take control of your money matters.

PROTECT YOURSELF AGAINST THE PROS

Whether you know it or not, you are already an investor. You make decisions every day about how you will invest your money and your time. Do you use money as a tool to enhance the quality of your life, or is it a more like a weapon that can harm you?

Increasing your financial awareness is how you protect your financial well-being. The banks, real estate agents, mortgage brokers, financial advisors, and insurance salespeople whom you deal with on a regular basis are armed with information and tools to maximize profits. Do you have an understanding of how they are paid for the products they sell to you? While they deserve to make a living for providing a service, it's a two-way street where you must benefit as well.

Take responsibility to educate yourself so others don't profit from your ignorance. Are you aware that the strategy of the many big banks is to the break the law intentionally, making sure that the profits are higher than the fine they have to pay if they get caught? There are actually job positions of people who calculate these risk ratios.

One of the biggest scams out there is your average mutual fund. After you pay hidden fees, almost all actively managed mutual funds underperform the market, providing an average return of 2 percent. After yearly 3 percent inflation, you're losing 1 percent per year on your investment. Institutions count on the fact that the majority of people are blind or simply not paying attention. Don't let that be you.

GOALS AND INVESTING

Learning about money is empowering. Whether you absorb knowledge by listening, reading, or doing, there are multitudes of ways to increase your financial IQ. Look for a platform that resonates with your learning style to avoid feeling overwhelmed or bored.

Financial podcasts are great because in addition to being informative, they're quite entertaining. If you love reading, there are literally thousands of books on the subject. There are even free online courses offered from top tier universities like Yale, MIT, and Purdue where you can acquire knowledge from the best finance minds in the world.

Other than the obvious, food and shelter, what are your finance goals for the short term and the long term? Are you planning for a retirement that allows you to travel while still earning income? Do you want to buy a house? Is it important to give your children the head start in life that you never had? Or do you want to fly on your own private jet?

The recipe for financial success is the same for everyone, and it's pretty simple. Spend less than you make, and invest the left-over money. Other than inventions, inheriting money, winning the lottery, or committing crimes, this is the only way to accumulate wealth, and it works for everyone. The greatest outcome of your financial success will be determined by how much you to choose to invest and what kind of investments you make.

BUY WHAT YOU KNOW

What should you invest in? What types of opportunities are right for you? Your chances for success will always be higher when you "buy what you know" and enter an area that holds your interest.

To succeed, you'll need to stay on top of trends and regulations and study how the major players in the field succeed. Avoid the temptation of getting involved in something where you have no control and no knowledge just because someone else made money doing it.

Financial guru Warren Buffett said it best: "Risk comes from not knowing what you're doing." Early in my investing career, I read a book by Jim Rogers about commodity investing. I admired him and his track record. Even though I knew nothing about commodities, and I had zero interest in learning about them, I invested $100,000 in his fund.

I lost over half the investment over four years before I decided to cut my losses. The most valuable thing I gained was the lesson of what not to do. Thankfully, it was early enough in my life to recover financially.

I used the remaining $50,000 to invest in an area where I am an expert. With my experience in interior design and my husband's expertise in construction management, investing in dilapidated rental properties, fixing them up, and using the income to buy more properties made much more sense for us. By investing in something we understand and love, we have generated millions of dollars of wealth.

THE RIGHT TIME TO BUY

Money is almost always made when you buy. Whatever you're buying—stocks, a business, real estate, or other investments—buy it when it's out of favor, when everyone else is selling. It's the most basic idea in the world, yet millions of people chase after investments when they have already run up in value. They go all-in when the smart money is about to sell.

All business goes in cycles, up and down. Study the pattern of your industry and where it is in the investment cycle. Some of the wisest investors in the world value capital preservation (not losing your money) over capital appreciation (earning more money). Dig deep for the courage and patience to wait for the right time. Losing 50 percent of your money makes it necessary to gain 100 percent back just to break even.

ACCUMULATING FOUND MONEY

Some of you are reading this and thinking, "I'm barely getting by, how will I ever be able to save anything to invest?" Start by saving the money that you might be throwing away without even knowing it.

Think about fees. How much money are you paying in late fees, early withdrawal fees, minimum balance fees, over the limit fees, high-percentage credit card interest fees, ATM fees, and management fees on investments? How much do they affect your bottom line every month?

Would opening an account at a local credit union instead of a bank save you thousands of dollars in fees? Are you paying monthly fees for services or products you don't need or use? Cancel them.

How many late fees are you incurring each month because you were distracted and forgot to pay a bill on time? Take a few minutes to avoid ever paying a late fee again by setting up automatic payments. Pay attention to fees and stop giving your hard-earned money away to make others rich. Add up all the money you would have paid in fees and memberships that you don't need or use and invest that money.

CREDIT SCORES MATTER

Another important reason to start paying your bills on time is to keep your credit score high. When you are delinquent on payments, your credit score takes a hit, and you end up paying higher interest rates on all of your home and car loans and credit cards. The difference between a mediocre score (600–720) and a great score (721–800+) could amount to hundreds of thousands of dollars over your lifetime.

When you pay down debt and make your payments on time, you increase your score. You're also entitled to a free report from each of the three main credit agencies each year. Get and check your reports to make sure they are valid and no one has stolen your identity (at www.annualcreditreport.com).

HOW MONEY MAKES MONEY

Learn about the power of compound interest and how it works for or against you. One of the best finance books I ever read was *5 Day Weekend: Freedom to Make Your Life and Work Rich with Purpose* by Garrett Gunderson and Nik Halik. The book focuses on the concept of compound interest and how it supercharges investments by growing them, which results in you having more money to invest.

The core principle of the book is that when you invest in income-generating ventures, you won't have to work forty-plus hours a week. Because your investments are making money for you, you can do more of the things that enrich your life. Sounds pretty great, right?

But compound interest can also work against you when you owe money. Every month that you carry a credit card balance, interest is added to the balance of what you owe. If you pay less than the interest charged, the amount you owe grows. Wouldn't you like to use that type of financial weaponry in your favor?

If you're saying to yourself, "But I can't afford to pay the full balance every month," then you're living beyond your means and you need to find ways to either cut expenses or earn more income.

THE AMERICAN DREAM IS ALIVE AND WELL

If you live in the United States and tell yourself that you have don't have the knowledge or money to invest, you're lying to yourself and letting fear get in the way of your success. Immigrants with next to nothing come to Western countries every day, pool their resources, and make life-changing investments for their future.

And it's not only immigrants. Anyone who is willing to educate him- or herself, take responsibility for their financial IQ, and work can and will succeed. Becoming a successful investor doesn't require a high-paying job, a college degree, or parents who help you financially. Although those things do make it easier, they are not barriers to entry.

Let me tell you a story about Karina. After dropping out of fashion school when she realized she didn't really like fashion and didn't want to incur $100,000 in debt, she decided to start a business, housecleaning for Airbnb owners. In a few short years, the woman who started out by cleaning my Airbnb units for $75 a day became the owner of her own business and began a career as a real estate investor.

Karina reached out to Airbnb owners and began building up enough steady units that she was able to hire a few people under her to help her clean.

She studied the process of successful Airbnb owners and the mistakes made by owners who failed. She offered her services as co-host on the rental site platforms, never asking to be paid. Instead, she gained insight as to how to manage the guests and became an expert in Airbnb policies.

Whenever she approached one of her owners with a question, she smiled with an attitude of gratefulness. We were all more than happy to answer her many questions about how the loan process worked and what metrics were needed for a good investment. While she saved money, she used her free time to research the best loan programs and areas with undervalued properties.

Eventually she had a down payment and the income to qualify for a loan. She recently purchased her first house, a small one-bedroom cottage. She plans to live in the front and convert the garage into a rental unit. This young lady is twenty-four years old and did it all by herself, starting with a job that only paid $75 per day. If she can do it, anyone can do it.

TEN YEARS FROM NOW, YOU'LL WISH YOU STARTED TODAY

If you haven't started already, now is the time to begin saving and investing. When you receive your next bonus or raise, put it into savings immediately. You won't notice any difference in your quality of life by saving that money, but it will change your life for the better as it grows.

Spend less than you make, pay off debts, and educate yourself about money and investments. There is free and plentiful information all over the internet and in libraries. Identify your financial goals so you can begin to meet them.

PROTECTING WHAT YOU'VE EARNED

Once you acquire assets—home, car, investments—you have something to lose. Make sure you are protected from unnecessary tax consequences and litigious people by meeting with an estate-planning attorney, an insurance agent, and a good tax adviser. The codes and laws are ever changing, complex, and nearly impossible to comprehend without the aid of professionals.

It seems like every time I have a meeting with my CPA, I learn about a new requirement. Because of that, successful finance strategies need to be fluid and adapt to the changes in regulations by your local, state, and federal governments. Having an awareness or basic understanding of these laws, and using them to your advantage, will help you make and retain more money.

You should never feel guilty about paying the least amount of taxes that you can. Always remember that the responsibility of a good citizen is to pay the minimum amount of tax required by law. Additionally, asset protection strategies like wills, trusts, and umbrella insurance policies safeguard your money and investments. These financial instruments give you peace of mind and control over the wealth that you have worked so hard to accumulate.

One last thing—if you go into business, any business, use a contract. Make sure it is written or reviewed by an attorney who specializes in the same field. Don't ever do business on a handshake. You will inevitably find yourself in a lawsuit, having done nothing to deserve it, but nonetheless you will be unable to protect yourself. It's a tragic outcome that is totally preventable.

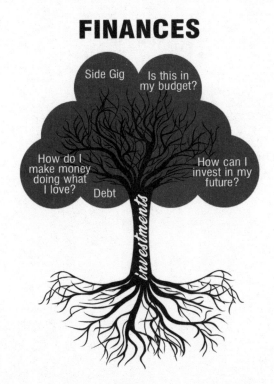

FINANCES

Side Gig

Is this in my budget?

How do I make money doing what I love?

Debt

How can I invest in my future?

investments

Where the
needs of the world
and your talent cross,

*there lies
your vocation.*

- Author Unknown

CHAPTER 6

Meaningful Work

Have you ever stopped to think about what you really want to do with the one life you have? The average person spends a quarter of their life working and studies show that 80 percent of people don't like their work. That means that the majority of working people in our society are unhappy for a good portion of their lives. What sets the other 20 percent of people apart?

To be fulfilled in life, you must do work that completes you, not depletes you. When you do what you love, you're good at it, and you can make a living doing it, you experience balance. We are often tempted to sacrifice our passions and beliefs in exchange for monetary rewards, which result in short-lived happiness and imbalance in the Finances Quadrant.

We are lucky to be alive in a time when we have choices of how to design our lives and do meaningful work. Will you choose to create a life that aligns with your talents, beliefs, and passions and that adds value to others' lives? When your life is over and someone tells your story, will it be the one you wished for or a heartbreaking compromise?

ALIGNING PASSION AND A PAYCHECK

The Japanese have a concept called *ikigai*. It refers to the things that make one's life worthwhile. The components of *ikigai* are four overlapping quadrants pertaining to work: what you love, what you're good at, what you can be paid for, and what the world needs. How can you combine those interests to hit all these points? Most people focus on the getting paid, thinking money will bring them happiness. But it's been proven time and time again, throughout history and across cultures, that this is not always true.

Harvard University is conducting a study about happiness that has gone on for over seven decades. The study has followed the lives of two groups of men from Boston. The first group comes from wealthy and privileged backgrounds. The second group grew up disadvantaged, in the worst slums of the city, many with parents who were abusive alcoholics.

Over the life of the study, some of the first group fell down the social ladder, while some from the second group climbed the ladder to great financial success. But the common thread in their primary reason for happiness or lack of happiness was not how well they did or did not do financially—it was the connection they had to other people. Across the board, without fail, their capacity for contentment was defined by the way their actions affected others.

MEANING OVER MONEY

There is a wave of thinking sweeping across our culture that places a higher value on individual creativity, meaning, and community than having tremendous amounts of wealth. Unfortunately, most of us don't have a strong conviction of exactly what meaningful work looks like. There's no lightning bolt of inspiration that lights up our perfect path.

Instead, we get occasional hints where we can tune into what we "like." Start to pay attention to those clues as you imagine what those "likes" would feel like as a career. This is called curiosity, and it's a feeling we tend to lose as we get set in our routines as we age.

Without the pressure to make money, children naturally gravitate toward what they enjoy doing. No child has ever answered the question of what they want to be when they grow up with "miserable for a quarter of my life." So ask yourself: *If money is not an issue, what do I want to be when I grow up?* What excites you and makes you lose track of time?

If you're stumped trying to answer that question, you're not alone.

WHAT YOU DO WELL AND LOVE DOING

Figuring out how to make your life's work meaningful may take a lot of time and self-reflection. Be patient and invest this time. Envision the type of life you would like to have. Start by writing down everything you love to do and everything you do well. Think about how you want to spend your days.

Would you love to be mobile and work from anywhere in the world? Do you get more satisfaction working on a team or working alone? Are you the type of person who needs to be supervised to be productive or are you self-motivated? Do you require outline and structure or do you do better being creative?

Is being active outdoors appealing to you or do you prefer to work indoors on computers? What activity do you do when time flies? What are you doing when you're in the flow? Leave money out of it because the concern about how we will get paid doing these things will stifle your creativity. Write down all the things you love in the "what you love" area of the *ikigai* symbol (there's a blank one at the end of the chapter, so fill it up).

What are you good at? What are your strengths? What do you do better than everyone else? Is there something that other people think you do exceptionally well? Do you do something that comes really easily to you, like a second nature? Write these things in the "What you're good at" oval in the *ikigai* symbol.

Do you see an overlapping of your skills (what you're good at) and interests (what you love)? It's important that you equally weigh these two sections. They're not the same thing. You may love cooking, but if you burn everything you make and nothing tastes good, it's probably not going to work out for you. The idea of being a concert pianist might be appealing, but it's not going to work if you aren't musically inclined.

THAT TIME I BECAME A STOCKBROKER

Likewise, stay away from things you do really well if you don't truly love them. When I graduated from college, I had no idea what I wanted to do. It was the late 1980s, when everyone worshiped money.

One of my parents worked on Wall Street. The topic of finance was routine dinner conversation at my house. I felt very comfortable discussing anything related to finance and money.

From the time I was a little kid, it was apparent that I was very good at the art of persuasion. The people around me put those two things together and suggested that I become a stockbroker. Not having a better plan, I went into to work as a stockbroker, or what they called a financial advisor, for Smith Barney.

Straight out of the gate, I outperformed thousands of others and became the number-one rookie for the firm. Soon thereafter I moved to Merrill Lynch, where I once again became one of the top-performing brokers in the entire company. I was making a bunch of money and people respected me.

The problem was that although I did enjoy putting points on the board and winning, I didn't find any satisfaction in what I was doing for a living. The hours were way too long, the job was never ending. Nothing I did felt tangible because I wasn't building anything other than more zeros on the ends of people's accounts. Being good at something isn't enough, and money is not meaning.

WHAT YOU STAND FOR

The next thing you want to examine is your values. Aligning your work with these values is a key part of job satisfaction. How do you define yourself? What are your needs? Is spending time to raise your children more important than a high-powered job that requires you to get a nanny?

Ask yourself: *What is important for me to accomplish before I die? Is it important that the people I work with share my beliefs?* Do you want to do work that benefits your community or a larger group of people? Is the idea of helping other people appealing to you?

Millions of people have found immense pleasure working for nonprofits or as social workers, firefighters, clergy, scientists, physicians, and teachers because they are able to see the impact they have on other people's lives. Is there a professional that represents who you are? What kind of mark do you want to leave on the world and your community? Write down the ideas that the world needs in your *ikigai* symbol.

GETTING PAID

Now you need to figure out how to make money doing something related to these three things. What professions exist that embody what you're passionate about, what you're good at, and what you love? If you're having a hard time imagining one, share your *ikigai* with a trusted friend or family member. The answers may be written on the page, but you may be so emotional about the outcome that they're hard to see.

You might also consider working with a career coach who will analyze the information and plot out potential careers that resonate with you. It's entirely possible that your perfect job doesn't exist yet and you will need to invent it. Author Jeff Goins describes this as the "Art of Work," viewing all of your work as an artist's portfolio.

Each seemingly separate skill and experience that you have weaves its way into a new career that uses all those strengths. This is a career that motivates and excites you. Think about a problem people have that is related to your love, your passion, and your talent. Could your abilities help to solve it?

INVENTING YOUR CAREER

Problems for others mean opportunities for you, and new industries are being born every day. Fifteen years ago, no one would have believed you could earn a living making silly home videos.

Penn Holderness and his wife Kim were struggling television personalities in New York City. Unable to support a family there, they made a move to Raleigh, North Carolina, where they could form a community of caring neighbors. To support themselves in their new town, Penn turned his talents for writing and producing music videos into an entirely new career.

He makes hilarious parody videos with his wife, two kids, and neighborhood friends. With many millions of views, the videos are so appealing, especially to families with children like theirs, that they been able to monetize their channel on YouTube. The videos have attracted thousands of advertisers, many of which have become clients.

Next in the works for the family is a reality show of what it's like behind the scenes of making these videos. The show will reveal how they juggle a growing business and family obligations. Here is a guy who loves production, is talented at making music and videos, had the desire to spend time doing something fun with his family and friends, and is able to make a living.

In the overcrowded space of entertainment, where everyone wants to be an actor or a musician, Penn Holderness exemplifies how you can discover your own path and create success. When you become aware of what is truly important to you, decide how you want to live, and have the courage to go for it, the possibilities are truly magical.

DEFINING SUCCESS

My definition of being a success at work comes from one of my interns, Simran. Many years ago, when she worked in my office, she spoke affectionately about a friend of hers who was also an interior designer. I had never heard of her friend and asked if the other designer was successful.

Simran replied, "If doing something you are passionate about and being able to make a living at it means you're successful, then yes, she is successful." This intern was in her early twenties and had already figured out one of the central keys to a balanced life. What she said was one of the most profound things I've ever heard.

It has been a beacon for the times I have had to make the tough decisions about the importance of money versus my peace of mind. It echoes in my head each time I contemplate whether I should engage in a lucrative opportunity that isn't the best fit for me professionally or personally.

You have to find what motivates you, the thing or things that make you want to get out of the bed in the morning, the thing you feel really good about doing. Search deep and reflect to discover your core competencies and what inspires you.

Examine your values. When you know how you want to live, you can live intentionally with purpose. Define what it will take to financially support that way of life and explore all the possibilities to make that plan a reality.

If the idea of trading financial security and status is less important than following your dreams, find time somewhere in your life to explore your passions. It's normal to desire material wealth and it's necessary to have the means to pay for expenses. But too many people wind up at the end of their lives filled with regret because they didn't spend their time on Earth doing something that really mattered to them.

The loss of spirit cannot be bought back. Time wasted wishing you did something else can never be recovered. Discover your bliss. Live your bliss.

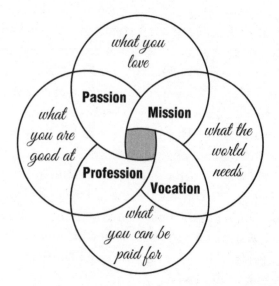

Risk Something

or forever sit
with your dreams.

– Herb Brooks

CHAPTER 7

Changing Careers

It's no surprise that more people are changing careers than ever before. Most of us have dreamed what it would be like to change our career to do something we enjoy more. It could be a sudden epiphany or years of built-up frustration that leads us to this point. Yet so many people, bound by fear of the unknown, stay stuck in careers that are unfulfilling.

Paralysis overcomes us when we envision a new career. Often, we think of all the reasons why trying something new won't work out for us. A playlist of fear-based questions runs through our minds. *How will I pay my bills? What else do I know how to do? After I throw it all away, will I even like the other career?*

Or someone tells you that you can't do it, and that you are insane to throw away a valuable job. But only you know when your life is out of sync because your work is no longer meaningful. Only you fully understand the depth of your passions, your tolerance for what you're going through, and the ideals that govern your life.

Sometimes it takes many years of life experience for that realization to occur; for some it comes right away. If you're contemplating taking that leap, you're not alone.

REASONS TO GO

Why are people willing to walk away from careers in which they have invested so much time and money?

The industry you work in may have changed so that you no longer have a job. Your personal and professional life may be completely out of balance, leaving you no time to spend with your family and friends. You may have been passed up one too many times for a promotion. Maybe you were fired. Maybe you're bored, work is tedious, and you aren't fulfilling your potential. Maybe you've reached the top and there's no more challenge to be had.

It could be time to retire from one field and explore another. You may develop a physical limitation, like an illness or injury, which makes your job uncomfortable. It might be an ethical issue; maybe the people you work with are criminals. You might just plain hate what you do. You're miserable and taking it out on people you love.

Your current career may not have been something you wanted to do in the first place. Influence from others, life circumstances, or the simple need to make money may have landed you in a profession where you feel stuck. If you're feeling sad, angry, resentful, or hopeless when you think of work, pay attention to these events and clues in your life. Don't settle. If you feel you can be or do something different, then do it, even if you're afraid.

UNCOMFORTABLE CHANGES

The magnitude of a career change is scary, a journey to the unknown. Although we crave personal growth and enrichment, our doubts and fears are stronger than our desire for self-actualization and genuine satisfaction. It's entirely possible that we will begin another career that is also a poor fit.

What if we start a new business and we fail? We worry about the time and financial investment we may have to make to enter a new profession. We don't want to look like losers who quit.

Starting over may seem too daunting. Doing something new is intimidating, but you should be terrified about wasting your life doing something that makes you unhappy. Unless you take the risk, the reward will never come.

Humans are born to make changes because our brains are wired to adapt. When we solve problems or challenges, our brains release endorphins, which make us feel great. The ability to figure new things out is an innate quality. Knowing the pitfalls, and focusing on the positive aspects, can help us move in the right direction as we make major changes in our lives.

FINANCIAL CONCERNS

Money fears are real. If you leave a well-paying job, you'd better make a plan for how to replace the money you need. If you don't have savings or someone who is willing to support you while you go through this transition, you'll need to get creative and make some sacrifices.

You can keep working while you transition. You might negotiate to work from home, using the commute time to work at another job. If you're starting a new business, consider going in with a partner you trust. If two people are responsible, there's someone else to share the work and financial burden.

In the following chapter about debt, there are a lot of strategies for saving money and reducing expenses. These tactics will come in handy if money is an issue in your career change. Planning a money-wise strategy will help to alleviate some of the stress surrounding your choice to start something new.

THE RIGHT QUESTIONS TO ASK

Knowing you want to do something and actually doing it are two different things. Once you know what you want to do, you need to ask yourself more practical questions.

- What kind of skills do I need?
- How much money and time do I have to invest?
- Is this a growing field?
- What is the lifestyle like in this new field?
- Do I need to relocate to do this?
- What kind of hours will I work?
- How much money can I expect to make?
- If I'm starting a business, what's the success rate for others?
- Are there things about this new job that will be the same things that made me unhappy in my old job?
- How am I going to get into this field?

WORKING YOUR OLD OR NEW NETWORK

Starting a new career will require a plan that starts with reaching out to existing connections and making new ones to gain exposure to leads, referrals, and information leading to your new career. First, talk to other people who have transitioned to new careers. You'll learn about their process and the steps they took to prepare for their new career. They'll give you the answers to questions swirling in your head. They will instill confidence in you. Seeing that they have done it helps us believe that we can do it too.

These may be the only people telling you to go for it, when others around you are reinforcing your fears. Avoid these "Debbie Downers" who say you're insane for leaving a well-paying job.

Don't be distracted by other people's idea of success. Listen to your gut.

If the people you know can't help you get into your new field, it's time to develop new networks. If you're not on LinkedIn, join and set up a profile. Start connecting with others in your new field.

People love to give advice. Speaking with people who are in the industry you want to join will ensure that what you learn about this new career is factual. Ask them what they don't like about their job and whether they would do it all again if they could start over.

Set up appointments with headhunters to verify everything you've learned in your research. Learn what specific skills and experience you need to land a job. Through these connections, discover opportunities for internships, shadowing, and volunteer positions.

TRANSITIONING WITHIN

You may not need to leave your industry altogether if there are parts about it that you still love. Is it possible for you to use the skills that you already have in a brand-new way, rather than leaving all your experience behind? Are you able to make a transition within your industry?

Here's how I did it. I've been emotionally charged about interior spaces, architecture, furnishings, and gardens since I was four years old. Making something ugly and underutilized reach its full potential has always been exhilarating for me.

Being a Type A personality, I decided to be one of the best interior designers in the world. I've accomplished that goal by working with some of the wealthiest people in the world, starring in an HGTV series called *Real Designing Women*, writing a bestselling book, *Green Interior Design*, and becoming the top design professional in my niche.

My award-winning work has been published in countless articles and books across the world. I have worked with some of the most established brands in the world, such as American Express, Volvo, and Verizon. But I was never been happy just being an interior designer.

As the years went by, I became more famous, more successful, and more unhappy. I don't like waste. I don't enjoy trashing perfectly usable things just to refill a home with new, coordinating items. Although I love the end result of building something from nothing or refurbishing the dilapidated, I knew that my purpose on Earth was more than making people's homes pretty and functional.

It's also challenging to work with clients who are slow and indecisive, because I move fast, I'm efficient, and making decisions comes naturally to me. Getting things done on time and on budget makes sense to me.

One of the drawbacks of being an interior designer involves waiting for other people to make up their minds, then change their minds, and then be unhappy when things cost more and take longer than their original plans. When I started to dread Monday morning, I knew it was time to change things. When I took an inventory of what gave me the most joy about my job, it was helping people live their best lives.

When I did my book tour for *Green Interior Design*, audience members always wanted to know how I created such a successful business. With the encouragement of my brother-in-law and the support of my husband, I started a conference called Design Camp, an online and in-person training program to help other professionals in my industry achieve the success I had experienced. Empowering thousands of people to thrive made me feel more alive than anything I have ever done.

In 2016, a publicly traded company bought Design Camp from my partners and me, and I have been longing for that sense of purpose ever since. And that's why you're reading this book. I'm pivoting again, by expanding my existing skills into a new market. How can you add up the pieces of knowledge you've attained and parlay your expertise into more gratifying work in the same or new industry?

TRYING SOMETHING NEW

Now that you've made the decision to do something else, you may experience a kind of identity crisis. You might be asking yourself, *If I didn't do this, who would I be?* When you've worked for years to become an expert who is respected by others, or feel that what you do defines who you are, it's tricky when you become something else.

If you stop doing that thing, do you stop being you? Of course not, but you will need to get comfortable being the student instead of the expert while you learn the ropes of your new career. Explaining your story may be a bit cumbersome too. You no longer identify as "Jodi the accountant," but you're not quite comfortable calling yourself "Jodi the artist" yet. The contradiction of old and new selves is uncomfortable, so give yourself time to be both until the new one really fits.

Maybe you are both, and it's perfectly fine to wear both hats and be both things. I'm fascinated by the term *multipotentialite*, coined by Emily Wapnick, which describes someone with many interests and creative pursuits. As opposed to a specialist who focuses on one career, a multipotentialite might be great at five or six different things and capable of excelling in all of them.

Have you ever been concerned about not being able to focus, like switching college majors or repeatedly doing something for a while and then wanting to change to something new? Have you, your parents, or your significant other been concerned because you never seem to find your one true calling? It's entirely possible you don't have just one—you have many.

Wapnick's take on this is that you might become bored because you've mastered the subject and it's time to move on to something new. Your strength may be the ability to fully absorb information faster than others and use your skills to innovate and problem-solve. If this sounds like you and you want to know more, check out her book, *How to Be Everything*.

NOT SETTLING

If and when the time comes when you want to try something fundamentally different that allows you to fulfill your passion, take advantage of your talents, and be aligned with your values, think about it long and hard. If you find yourself daydreaming about a completely new career and you have the will, a plan, the financial capability, and the courage to reinvent yourself, then my advice is to stop dreaming and go for it. You are the driver; you have the power to fill your work life with excitement and purpose.

Don't allow your fear to take over. Don't allow the fact that you already invested so much in something else stop you. Did you know that medicine is the profession with the highest percentage of career changes? Can you image spending hundreds of thousands of dollars and twelve years studying after high school only to discover that it's the wrong career for you?

Do you remember Mr. Chow from the *Hangover* movies? He was played by Ken Jeong, who was a doctor at Kaiser Permanente before he left it all to be a comedian. If you don't know anyone else who made a successful career change, you can watch his stand-up special on Netflix, *You Complete Me, Ho*, and get pumped up about trying something new. That second career sure worked out pretty well for him.

Your time on this planet is finite and you deserve to be happy. Is it time to make a career change?

CAREER WITHOUT DIRECTIONS

The average American has been in the same job for 9.88 years, rising to a substantial 13.91 years for professionals over the age of 55.

OPPORTUNITY

DEAD-END JOB

CAREER

VACANCY

22%
say that they "fell" in to their job rather than actively choosing

23%
"say that they feel like they are 'on a treadmill going nowhere.'"

AMERICANISM:
Using Money
you haven't earned
to buy things
you don't need
to impress people
you don't like.

- Robert Quillen

CHAPTER 8

Consumerism and Debt

If you've ever toured a home built before 1927, you might find that the closets are pretty small. That's because before this time, the average person in Western culture bought what he or she needed. A closet usually consisted of two or three work outfits and something nice to wear to their place of worship.

It was right around this time that the "father of public relations," Edward Bernays, nephew of Sigmund Freud, got together with some bankers and strategists to completely change the buying habits of Western civilization. Their goal was to create a culture of consumerism, transforming the populace into one that made purchasing decisions based on desire, rather than needs.

FROM NEED TO WANT

Paul Mazur, a leading Wall Street banker, has been quoted as saying, "People must be trained to desire, to want new things, even before the old have been entirely consumed. Man's desires must overshadow his needs." Advertising was radically altered to stop pointing out the benefits of a product and instead make you lust for it, just for the sake of having it. Commercials were designed to make you feel that you were inadequate or that you were missing out if you didn't buy the products.

This period in history spawned a mass consumer society. In the late 1970s, credit card companies realized that they could finance these desires, charge interest on the purchases, and earn tremendous profits from consumer debt. This was the beginning of the "credit expansion," and most Americans have been accumulating debt ever since.

AIRBRUSHED LIFESTYLES

If you pay attention to advertisements, you're at risk of being manipulated into buying things that "make you feel good about yourself," a mentality that puts about 40 percent of Americans into credit card debt. Advertisers dictate what it means to be successful. Luxury cars, constant technology upgrades, expensive vacations, outrageously priced fashion and jewelry—most of which are cheaply made in Chinese factories—are prevalent in all media, including social media.

The things that are shown to you on Instagram pages (and other forms of advertisements) are fake or curated, and the people who run such pages only present what advertisers want you to see. The reality is edited, and much of it doesn't make the cut. However, these images, this imagined life, has immense power over you, making you feel like everyone else has something and you're being left out.

Then you wind up spending money that you haven't yet made to keep up with something that isn't even real. This behavior is described as the psychology of status, where you want to measure up to people who are perceived to be "just a little better" than you. When they get something new like a car, you feel like you need one too. They buy a designer purse, and then you are compelled to drop a few grand on one as well, even though you know you will go into debt to have it. Let's just call it what it really is: envy.

We've all been trained to look up one level and attain the things those people have. The desire to move up, do better, and buy more things is how personal debt keeps growing. It does a double whammy of also ruining our planet due to overproduction and pollution. Is all of it really necessary?

EGO-BASED BUYING

So many people are paying down five-figure credit card balances for items that will soon become worthless, instead of investing in their futures. Why do we feel we need these things to be successful? If wearing that expensive watch, driving that luxury car, and walking around in designer clothing is making you go into debt, you are the opposite of successful. You've been brainwashed and knocked out of equilibrium.

When you buy things that you really don't need and can't afford, you're preventing yourself from having fiscal wellness and putting your Finances Quadrant into a tailspin. In addition to showing off, most of this behavior is driven by envy, competitiveness, boredom, depression, and even spite. Communication skills have completely broken down when someone spends money they don't have just to make their partners pay attention and get a reaction from them.

If you are intentionally spending money on frivolous things that result in being in debt, stop. If you think you will feel better if you have more, you won't. I've seen plenty of people with three or four walk-in closets filled to the brim, and they still aren't happy.

It is liberating to learn how to be comfortable with what you have and who you are. If you want more, then you need to figure out what steps to take to make more to pay for it. Figure out what really matters in your life and don't base it on what others have. When you do that, you may realize it isn't a bunch of stuff—it's surely not being in debt.

GETTING HELP

For some it's not about showing off—it's more of an acute problem or an actual illness. You may have been blindsided by a job loss or set back financially by a divorce, or you may be in student debt. Sadly, some live within their means and one emergency or health situation spirals them into debt.

If your spending is completely out of your control, you may have a real addiction to shopping. I'm not talking about a cute bumper sticker or a coffee mug that says "I'm a shopaholic." I'm talking about a bona fide compulsion where you can't stop buying things you don't need. If that's you, there's a group for this called Debtors Anonymous (DA). Their meetings are filled with some of the highest earners in North America sitting right next to people who make minimum wage. DA is also for anyone experiencing debilitating debt issues like student loans, business losses, or upside-down mortgages.

It can be embarrassing to admit you're in debt and difficult to talk to anyone about it because we are largely defined by our financial status. No matter why you're in debt, you'll need to get to the root cause and deal with it. Even if you somehow get out of debt, if you don't address the original reason you were in it, you'll likely wind up there again.

KNOWING THE NUMBERS

What strategies can you use to get out of debt? First, you have to identify exactly how much money you make each month and exactly how much you spend. Make a budget of every single expense you have, every dime you spend.

Until you know exactly what you're making and spending, you cannot assess where to eliminate spending to reallocate that money toward paying off your debt. Below are categories where most people spend and suggestions on how to cut back on these expenses.

Health Care: Health Insurance, Doctor Visits, Prescriptions, Supplements, etc.

Staying healthy by reducing stress, eating right, and exercising will reduce spending in this category. We discuss all of these throughout this book. Meaningful work, fiscal responsibility, wellness, and spirituality are all intertwined and have a profound impact on your health. If this category is one of your biggest spends, it can become less of a burden as you balance your quadrants.

Food: Groceries, Coffee Shops, Restaurants, Deliveries, Bars, Celebrations, etc.

Reduce eating out and completely eliminate buying waters and coffees on the go. It's about five times more expensive to buy prepared food and drinks than to make it yourself. You're also adding to the pollution of our planet with plastic water bottles and trash from coffee cups and to-go containers.

Fill up a water bottle and a thermos of coffee at home. If you're a coffee snob, learn how to make it exactly how you like it. For tea drinkers—even easier—boil some water, put it in a thermos, and bring your favorite tea bag. Eating out often also affects your health.

Add it up: $40/month on coffee + $300/month on eating out = $4,080/year.

Personal Care: Hair, Nails, Massages, Gym Memberships, Dry Cleaning, Shoe Shines, Skin and Body Products, Makeup, etc.

When we look good, we feel good. Taking care of our bodies and appearance is necessary, but overspending isn't.

Examine where you can cut back in this category. Have an unused gym membership? Kill it, or consider a less expensive workout option. YouTube has every kind of training you can imagine.

If working out is social for you, make a date with a friend and work out together. Find less expensive solutions for body, hair, and nail products. The truth is that most of the products, from high-priced to low, have the identical ingredients. You're paying for the advertising and marketing campaigns of products, not the quality.

Add it up: $100/mo. gym = $1,200/year.

Vacations and Entertaining

Try a staycation, where you do fun things locally. So many cities have free concerts, free museum days, and parks and outdoor spaces you can enjoy for free. Rediscover nature and go camping. Or skip hotels and use more reasonable Airbnbs.

Spend $5,000 less on your vacation = $5,000/year.

Housing

If your housing costs are killing you, it's time to go old-school and live the way our grandparents did when there were many people under one roof. Rent out rooms full-time or on vacation/event rental sites like Airbnb or Peerspace.

Turn off your air conditioner and use a fan; sweating is really good for you. Turn off the lights; take a shorter shower. Wear a sweater when it's cold instead of pumping the heat.

Start gardening, which includes the added bonus of exercising and getting outside. Clean your own house and walk your own dog. These cutbacks might sound silly, but they work.

Add it up: $30/month utilities + $400/month renter + $200/month housekeeper = $7,560.

Cutting back on just a few key areas in your life could save you almost $18,000 per year. It adds up fast!

Transportation

If you're in a high-cost monthly car loan or lease and you can't get out, consider joining a car sharing service like Turo for the days you don't need a car. On average, if you share your car nine days a month, you can cover a luxury car payment.

Fashion, Technology Items, Furnishings, and Any Other Nonessentials

Stop buying things you don't need. If you absolutely need something, try to buy it used. There are plenty of people selling things in almost brand-new condition for a fraction of the price you would pay for the same brand-new item.

Reselling comes in handy especially for children's items, like strollers, furniture, clothing, and toys, which are often in almost new condition when you no longer need them. (Though, certain items, such as cribs and car seats, ought to be purchased brand-new every time, per recommendations from national safety advisories.) Better yet, check sharing platforms. Buying used and sharing has the added benefit of helping to eliminate waste and pollution.

College or University

If you or your child is headed for college and there's a need to take out loans to pay for it, does attending a less expensive community college for the first two years make more sense?

By starting community college the summer after twelfth grade through a two-year period, you can work part-time and rack up two years of credits at community college prices before transferring to a four-year college to complete your degree. This will save you tens of thousands of dollars in tuition fees. You still get to graduate from a more prestigious school. No one cares where you went at the beginning. Additionally, you may be able to get into a better school this way, because students at the four-year school may have dropped out after the first or second year, leaving a spot for you.

You might consider not going to college at all, unless your job path absolutely requires it. You really need to do the math and some soul searching to know if it's worth going into debt for the degree you'll earn. The future job market will not value today's educational accomplishments the way people do now. The goal of college is to become well rounded, and with the internet most of the information can be had for free.

Downsizing and Cutting Expenses

If you're in major debt and the above reductions are merely a drop in the bucket, start selling assets that aren't essential. Is there anything you aren't using that has any value, such as a second home, a boat, jewelry, art, furniture, or clothing? Depending on its value, you can use a broker, or go to auction. For lower-priced items, put them up for sale online or have a yard sale.

Whether you're in debt or not, always shop for the best rates on all your credit cards, home loans, insurance policies, car loans, student loans, health insurance, cable, and internet and phone package. When you find a better deal, ask your current lender or provider to match it. Don't be afraid to leave them if they say no. Rates matter, just like fees, and they can mean the difference of hundreds of thousands of dollars over your lifetime.

Cutting expenses might not be enough to get you out of debt. You may want to consider a new job that pays more, or temporarily taking on an additional part-time job. At the end of this chapter, there is a more comprehensive budgeting form to help you identify all potential expenses you have. Fill it out and see where you're at so you can decide on the right action course to get out of debt. Even if you are debt free, it's a great exercise to see where you're spending money and identify ways you can capture more of your income for investments.

Staying Out of Debt

Using an app to record your spending and savings is a great way to be accountable and stay on track with your debt pay-down plan. Once you get out of debt, a budgeting app can help you control future spending and investing. Some of my favorites are Mint, PocketGuard, and YNAB (You Need a Budget).

Mint is the most comprehensive and complex, offering budgeting, categorizing of your expenditures, bill pay, fee alerts, and credit score watch. It's also tied to your bank and brokerage accounts.

PocketGuard links all your financial accounts, tracking income, savings, and bills throughout the month. It analyzes your bills and searches for ways for you to save money on better available deals.

YNAB (You Need a Budget) avoids full-blown budgeting, instead helping users to allocate money to bill paying, savings, or investing. The app style is playful, but using it produces serious results.

Stop spending more than you make, unless you are acquiring debt that provides potential for appreciation or income, like real estate or your own business. When you're in debt for frivolous consumer goods, you become a slave mentally and financially.

You cannot chart your own financial destiny and obtain balance when creditors bind you. Stop making yourself a victim of seductive advertisements; those companies don't care about you. Stop being prey for creditors. Their main goal is to get you and keep you in debt. Practice self-control and the art of window-shopping, because the truth is that you don't need all that stuff.

MONTHLY BUDGET WORKSHEET

CATEGORY	MONTHLY BUDGET	MONTHLY ACTUAL	DIFFERENCE
Income			
Monthly Pay (After Taxes)			
Alimony/Child Support Received			
Other Income			
Other Income			
TOTAL MONTHLY INCOME			
Expenses: Housing			
Mortgage or Rent			
Real Estate or Property Tax			
Personal Property Tax			
Homeowner's or Renter's Insurance			
Homeowner's Association or Condo Fees			
TOTAL HOUSING			
Expenses: Utilities			
Electric			
Gas			
Water/Sewage			
Trash			
Telephone			
Cell Phone			
Internet			
Cable TV			
TOTAL UTILITIES			
Expenses: Health/Medical			
Medical Insurance			
Dental Insurance			
Doctor Visits/Lab*			
Dentist*			
Orthodontist*			

CATEGORY	MONTHLY BUDGET	MONTHLY ACTUAL	DIFFERENCE
Therapist*			
Ophthalmologist/Glasses*			
Hospital/Emergency*			
Other			
TOTAL HEALTH/MEDICAL			
Expenses: Transportation			
Car Payments			
Car Insurance			
Car Maintenance/Repair*			
Mass Transit			
Gas			
Parking/Tolls			
Registration/Inspection*			
TOTAL TRANSPORTATION			
Expenses: Credit Cards, Loans, Other Expenses			
Credit Card: Balance:			
Credit Card: Balance:			
Credit Card: Balance:			
Student Loans			
Legal Fees			
Alimony/Child Support Paid			
TOTAL CREDIT CARDS, LOANS, OTHER			
Expenses: Food & Entertainment			
Groceries			
Meals Out			
Entertainment			
Hobbies			
Streaming Services			
TOTAL FOOD & ENTERTAINMENT			
Expenses: Children			
Child Care			
School Tuition			

QUADRANT LIFE

CATEGORY	MONTHLY BUDGET	MONTHLY ACTUAL	DIFFERENCE
Lunch Money			
School Supplies			
Extracurriculars/Sports			
Personal Grooming			
New Clothes			
Allowances			
Other			
TOTAL CHILDREN			
Expenses: Personal			
Dry Cleaning/Laundry			
Personal Grooming			
New Clothes			
TOTAL PERSONAL			
Expenses: Savings & Large Expenses			
Savings Going to an Account			
Gifts			
House Maintenance/ Repairs*			
Furniture*			
Charity*			
Vacation*			
TOTAL SAVINGS & LARGE EXPENSES			
TOTAL MONTHLY INCOME			
TOTAL MONTHLY EXPENSES			
TOTAL DIFFERENCE			
MONTHLY BUDGET			

*Expenses that you can budget for, so you have money saved for unplanned or annual bills.

BUDGET BREAKDOWN

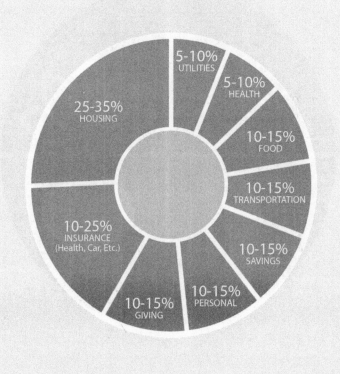

PART III

WELLNESS

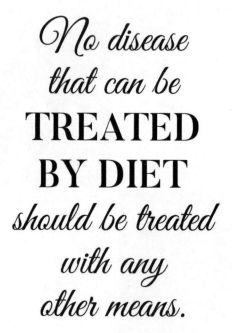

*No disease
that can be*
**TREATED
BY DIET**
*should be treated
with any
other means.*

- Moses Maimonides

CHAPTER 9

Diet and Disease Prevention

It's what you do every day that affects your health. Likewise, your health affects how you feel every day. What you eat plays an enormous role in role in your health, how you feel now, and how you will age.

Is your diet promoting illness or wellness? For too many people, the answer is illness. When we are ill, the body and mind do not function properly, which negatively affects every other quadrant and lowers our life quality. Chronic metabolic illnesses or "lifestyle illnesses," like type 2 diabetes, cardiovascular diseases, and strokes, have become a major health concern in Western societies and in the world's largest cities. Ninety-five percent of these diseases can be prevented and reversed by just by a change in diet.

MY JOURNEY TO WELLNESS

I want to start by saying that I'm not a doctor or a dietitian. But I have learned a lot about being well after a debilitating condition I experienced in the winter of 2011, which led me on an extensive journey of learning how diet affects our health. It only took me a few months to recover, but what I learned and continue to learn has had an unbelievable impact on my health. For the last eight years I have not been sick: not a cold, not a fever, and I do not take any pharmaceutical medicines.

I have always been physically fit and generally very healthy. But that all changed in February 2011 when I went to bed feeling great and woke up the next morning feeling like I had aged a hundred years in my sleep. Literally every single joint in my body was in pain. It hurt terribly to put weight on my feet and walk to the bathroom.

I took some Advil, searched online to see if something matched my symptoms (nothing did), and made an appointment with the first doctor available in my insurance network. He gave me a cortisone shot and I felt better. Two days later it was back again. I could barely walk, I couldn't lift my arms over my head, and I was uncomfortable in every position, whether lying, standing, or sitting.

I took some more Advil and made an appointment to see a Western doctor at a university hospital in Los Angeles. He did some tests, and even though the results came back negative for everything, he was sure I had rheumatoid arthritis (RA). I read the symptoms for RA, and they didn't match mine.

I explained this to him, yet he insisted that I needed to begin therapy for RA that would require me to take immune system–suppressing drugs and visit his office every three weeks (forever) to test my blood. He told me that I would need to be on this medication for the rest of my life. Even if I ever felt better, I should not stop taking it because the disease could come back and the symptoms would be worse.

I had never been on any prescription medication, and I was devastated. This medicine literally shuts down your immune system, which would likely cause you to develop an array of other illnesses. I researched the drug on the Centers for Disease Control site. It had a huge red warning about this drug saying that unless your life was in danger, you should avoid taking it.

I decided against taking the drug. That was the last Western doctor I ever visited. (Since then I've discovered pharmaceutical companies exert a remarkable amount of influence on Western doctors, beginning in their formative medical school years.)

Months went by and I researched every natural remedy that I could find. I learned that sugar, refined starches (like chips, bread, white rice), milk products, alcohol, and meats all caused inflammation. I removed all of them from my diet. Although it's not known to be inflammatory, I also stopped drinking caffeine.

I allowed only nourishing and detoxifying foods into my daily diet, such as noni juice, raw turmeric, ginger, and shiitake mushrooms. I ate mostly vegetables, fruits, nuts, seeds, and whole rice—all organic. I ate plenty. I was never hungry. I lost a lot of weight, but I was still in the same amount of pain. (If you're looking for a diet to help shed some pounds, this one does the trick.)

Even though the pain was so intense that I cried every night trying to fall asleep, I quit taking Advil. By chance I was introduced to a naturopath who ran his own tests. His diagnosis was that extremely resilient bacteria had entered my bloodstream and were causing symptoms in line with some autoimmune diseases. My white blood cells were in a battle with the bacteria. I simply needed to get the bacteria out of my body.

Because I had cleansed my body with a clean diet for the prior few months, I was in prime condition to be cured. He suggested taking daily doses of colloidal silver, a natural antibiotic, organic sulphur, and thirty minutes in a sauna or thirty minutes in an Epsom salt bath every day. In three weeks I was cured. I had zero pain in my joints. I don't know where I picked up that bacteria, but I know that what I ate helped to cure me.

WESTERN DIET DISEASE

If you're interested in preventing disease, maintaining a healthy body, or reversing damage that you may have done, you have to examine what you're eating and how it affects you. Most people in North America and Europe are eating a Western diet that consists largely of processed foods. If it comes in a package, and it's not dried whole grains, beans, or rice, it's probably processed.

So many processed foods are devoid of the nutrients that our bodies need and they are filled with sugars, chemicals, and bad fats. My tiny pantry now consists of only six shelves that are two feet long, and half of it has cat food and water bottles on it. Most of what I eat needs to be prepared, and not in a microwave. I gave up the microwave a long time ago and it has been a large factor in my weight being the same as it was in high school.

If I want to eat something, I have to want it so much that I am willing to take the time to prepare it. When I want a quick snack, it's usually a piece of fruit, a vegetable, a handful of nuts, or a little piece of cheese, because I don't have any prepackaged "goodies" in my house.

So what is about the Western diet that's so bad?

Sugar

The Western diet has too much sugar for our body to process, and not enough fiber. Sugar is addictive. It releases dopamine, which makes us feel euphoric.

The more sugar we eat, the more we want that feeling of euphoria. When you get in a cycle of wanting sugar all the time, it's like being a drug addict. But sugar is legal—you can buy it anywhere, and it's socially acceptable to eat all day.

When you eat sugar without fiber, like candy, sodas, juices, cookies, or cakes, you're eating simple carbohydrates. Without fiber, you don't get filled up because the food gets absorbed too quickly. Your blood sugar level spikes. The pancreas secretes insulin to bring the blood sugar back down to a healthy level. The rush of insulin accelerates the conversion of calories into fat.

A high insulin level is the reason why two-thirds of Americans are overweight. It's not how much you eat; it's what you're eating. Processed food is so high in sugar that average insulin levels are three times higher than forty years ago, which leads to a condition called insulin resistance, which leads to type 2 diabetes.

More than ninety million people in the United States have type 2 diabetes (or prediabetes), a disease that, in many cases, may be cured by changes in diet. There's a 70 percent increase in children with diabetes over the last four decades. These kids are inundated with sugar; it's everywhere, all the time, in everything they eat.

If you want to set your children up for good dietary habits, don't reward them with sugary treats. Instead, write them a special letter telling them you're proud of them, or spend time doing something they choose, like playing a board game.

Omega-3 Fatty Acids

Western diets don't contain enough omega-3 fatty acids. Eating foods or supplements that contain omega-3 fatty acids boosts neurogenesis, the formation of new cells. This also helps prevent heart disease, strengthen eye health, reduce risk of breast and colon cancer, and fight anxiety and depression. Foods like cold-water wild fish, pasture-raised eggs, and avocados are incredibly important for your body and brain.

Micronutrients

People are not eating enough organic, micronutrient-rich fruits and vegetables. Micronutrients are how you get the vitamins and minerals for energy production, immune function, blood clotting, bone health, and fluid balance. They also contain antioxidants, which fight inflammation and neuroinflammation (inflammation in the brain).

Branch Chain Amino Acids

A Western diet is lacking in branch chain amino acids found in foods like brown rice, chickpeas, almonds, lentils, wild fish, pasture-raised beef, chicken, and eggs. Branched chain amino acids increase muscle growth, reduce exercise fatigue, and prevent muscle degeneration.

Trans Fats

There are too many trans fats in a processed food diet. Trans fats make food stay crisp and crunchy and able to stay on grocery store shelves longer. Trans fats increase your risk of developing inflammation, type 2 diabetes, heart disease, and stroke. Some of these foods include blended vegetable oils; fried salty foods like chips, crackers, biscuits cookies, and movie popcorn; doughnuts; deep-fried foods like French fries; frozen food like chicken and fish fingers; packaged cake mixes; and nondairy coffee creamers.

Omega-6 Fatty Acids

Western diets contain too much omega-6 fatty acids, which are found in cheap, processed vegetable oils, leading to inflammation of the brain, cancers, rheumatoid arthritis, and depression. Don't confuse these with omega-9 essential fatty acids, found in foods like extra virgin olive oil, nuts, and sesame oil. These types of foods, in moderation, are good for you.

When we consume a lot of these types of foods, they promote inflammation of the brain, which compromises neurons' ability to connect properly. This inflammation negatively affects the memory center of the brain, the hippocampus. When the hippocampus is damaged from inflammation, the signals that are supposed to tell the stomach that you're full don't connect properly. When you don't feel satiated, you eat more of the foods that cause the damage to the hippocampus. The more unhealthy things you eat, the worse your health becomes.

Dining Out

I'm not saying you should never have a cookie or French fries again, but these foods need to be consumed infrequently, not as the majority of your diet. The same goes for eating in restaurants. With very few exceptions, restaurants use the lowest-quality food they can get away with, augmenting it with saturated fat and sodium to make it taste good. They're in business to make money, not keep you healthy.

Even eating in most vegan or vegetarian restaurants doesn't mean the food is healthy. They can still use cheap oils and non-organic produce laden with pesticides. Unless you know the chef, own the restaurant, or make it yourself, you don't know what you're eating.

If the social aspect of dining out is important for you, invite people over for dinner or drinks. Cooking together is good for relationships, your finances, and your health. It's easier than ever to cook at home with meal kit delivery services. They drop off boxes with pre-measured, prepped organic ingredients and all you have to do is follow their step-by-step directions. Most meals take about thirty minutes to put together.

WHY ORGANIC

Why do I keep putting the word "organic" next to everything? First let's define what *organic* means. The USDA defines organic food as the product of a farming system that avoids the use of man-made fertilizers, pesticides, growth regulators, and livestock feed additives. Irradiation and the use of genetically modified organisms (GMO) are generally prohibited by organic legislation.

Nonorganic fruits and vegetables contain pesticides, which cause a number of health problems and are directly linked to many cancers and digestive and respiratory diseases. People complain that organic food is more expensive, but you will pay now or you will pay later with your health. If you choose in-season foods and skip the prepackaged items, you'll probably notice there's no change in your grocery bill.

EAT MORE PLANTS

There are a lot of ideas about the right way to eat for optimal health. Each body and lifestyle is different. You need to do the research and select the one that works for you. Whether vegan, vegetarian, keto, paleo, or the starch diet, the evidence is that eating organic plants is healthy.

The more plants you eat, and the less of other stuff, the longer you are going to live. Eating fresh, organic fruits and vegetables from a local garden is one of the best ways to get nutrient-rich vitamins and minerals. Foods that don't have to travel thousands of miles can be picked closer to the time that they are riper and more nutritious. They don't need to be picked prematurely and sprayed with gases to keep them from rotting on long journeys.

Farmers markets are a great source for fresh produce. It's also very gratifying to eat something you grew yourself. If you have some space in own yard or you can get a plot in a community garden, it's an incredible way to eat delicious food and hit all four quadrants.

Wellness comes from eating vine-ripened, in-season fruits and vegetables. Gardening together can strengthen relationships.

Working in a community garden is a way to meet people and even find Mr. or Mrs. Right. Organic farmers market food isn't cheap, so growing some of your own food could save you a few bucks. Being in touch with nature by growing what sustains you with the elements of sun, water, and soil is about as spiritual as it gets! If garden space is not available to you, anyone can grow potted tomatoes on a balcony, or fresh herbs like basil or mint in front of a window.

I live in Los Angeles in an average-size home. Instead of planting grass, we allocated some space to a growing a few varieties of fruits and vegetables, and we have two sweet hens that roam the yard, giving us natural fertilizer for our plants and fresh eggs every day.

ANIMAL PROTEIN

If you're a meat eater, you should consider two things about mass-produced meat: factory farms and pollution. It's not healthy to eat animals that are pumped up with antibiotics because they live in conditions so cramped and filthy that without the antibiotics, they'd die. If you don't care about the animal welfare aspect, consider your own health.

After energy production, factory farms are the second biggest contributor to greenhouse gases, land degradation, and water pollution. If you are going to eat animals, eat only healthy, pasture-raised animals that are consuming the foods that nature designed for them to eat. The same goes for fish: eat only wild-caught. Farm-raised fish is more likely to be raised in polluted, diseased, parasite-ridden water and treated with antibiotics. Most restaurants are serving factory-farmed meat and eggs.

Most lifestyle diseases (cardiovascular, diabetes, etc.) can be prevented or cured by a change in diet. Even your doctor will admit that you can heal some illnesses if you simply stop doing what is causing them. If you want to help prevent disease and maintain good health, stop eating processed foods and start preparing organic whole foods at home as the majority of your diet.

MY FAVORITES

Here's a bonus list of some of the things I take to stay healthy or when I'm feeling a little run-down. They work for me, but I encourage you to check with your health care provider to see if they are right for you.

Organic Sulphur

Herbicides, pesticides, and industrial farming have stripped the soil of adequate amounts of sulphur. It's a mineral we used to get naturally from our fruits and vegetables. Sulphur promotes oxygenation in the cells and aids in waste removal. The oxygen is necessary for cellular regeneration, which is how the body stays healthy and is able to combat disease.

Referred to as the beauty mineral, it aids in healthy skin and nails and clear skin tone and texture. Sulphur is important for forming collagen synthesis (the protein found in connective tissue) and repairing cell damage. It combats arthritis symptoms, giving joint pain relief. It breaks up scar tissues by flushing out acidic waste stored in cell tissues, fights inflammation, and promotes heavy metal detoxification and mental clarity. I take this every day.

Colloidal Silver

This is a solution of silver particles in a liquid base. In test tubes, the presence of colloidal silver near a virus, fungi, or bacteria cuts off its oxygen metabolism, effectively cutting off the lung of the pathogen. It's been banned by the FDA as a drug. As a food supplement, it's known to boost immunity.

The jury is out on whether colloidal silver is safe or toxic. It has been said to create a problem for the absorption of pharmaceutical medication, which isn't a problem for me because I don't take any. Colloidal silver has been used for thousands of years to treat infections, and it has worked for me personally. I take it on a daily basis to prevent inflammation and infection.

Interesting folklore: Throughout history, royalty have eaten with silver utensils. The daily trace amount of silver that was ingested from eating with the utensils has been said to give them "blue blood." These people generally seemed to have much longer life spans than the people who ate from lead-based utensils and plates. (Of course, the wealthy also enjoyed many privileges that contributed to their longevity: access to higher-quality food, less strenuous labor, cleaner living conditions, access to medical care, and so on.)

Colostrum (Bovine)

A nutrient-rich fluid produced in the breasts of female mammals, it's loaded with immune-growth and tissue-repairing properties. It has high levels of antibodies to boost the immune systems of newborn babies and protect them from infections. I use it when I feel run-down or like I might get sick. I take a few sprays a few times a day, and I never wind up getting sick.

Vitamin D

We don't go outside enough, where sunlight promotes vitamin D production in our body. The main function of vitamin D is to keep bones and teeth strong. It also promotes proper functioning of muscles, legs, heart, and brain. I take liquid vitamin D drops every day.

Vitamin C

This is good for collagen formation, wound healing, and repair and maintenance of cartilage, bones, and teeth. It's also said to help fight or lower the risks of getting colds, asthma, bronchitis, cardiovascular disease, cataracts, and cancer. I take liposomal vitamin C a few times a week, when I feel like I'm getting sick, or when I travel.

Organic Green Tea

This type of tea contains bioactive compounds that improve brain function and increase fat burning and physical performance, and antioxidants that may lower the risk of cancer. I drink it in the afternoon because it fills me up and fights sugar cravings.

Turmeric

This root has antioxidant and anti-inflammatory properties. It can contribute to healthy digestion. I take it daily.

TIPS TO EATING CLEAN

COOK YOUR OWN FOOD

READ THE LABELS

EAT WHOLE FOODS

EAT 5-6 MEALS A DAY

EAT BALANCED MEALS

AVOID PROCESSED FOODS

REDUCE OR ELIMINATE MEAT

REDUCE OR ELIMINATE DAIRY

MINIMIZE EXTRA FATS, SALTS & SUGARS

DON'T DRINK YOUR CALORIES

Those Who Think They Have
no time for
bodily exercise
Will Sooner or Later Have to Find Time for
illness.

- Edward Stanley

CHAPTER 10

Fitness

For about 300,000 years, humans have been active beings. Our bodies were made to move and be outdoors. Walking, running, hunting, gathering, farming, labor, and even ritual dancing comprised the majority of daily life. Since the Industrial Revolution, movement and amount of time spent outdoors has significantly decreased in developed nations.

Vehicles and mass transit are used instead of walking or horse or bike riding. Manufacturing and cultivation of agriculture, once done by hand, is largely done with machines. Most people now spend most of their time indoors, in front of screens. It's completely unnatural for humans to sit more than they move. Doing so puts you at risk of a long list of illnesses. Point blank, if you want to be in balance, with a healthy body, you need to move your body on a regular basis. Go play outside!

SITTING IS THE NEW SMOKING

In the last forty years, technology has made us more sedentary than at any other time in our existence. We have a sitting epidemic.

Technology has increased the number of jobs that require sitting all day in front of a screen and keyboard. It's turned learning, and entertaining ourselves, into sedentary activities.

You might be thinking: how can sitting possibly be bad for you? It's harmful to our bodies because when we sit for very long periods, we tend to slump over. This puts pressure on the lungs, and we don't take full breaths. Breathing is how we move oxygen around the body. Oxygen chemically converts our food into energy that the body uses to repair cells, muscles, and our brains and nerves, and to cleanse the body.

Sitting for long periods also reduces blood flow to the body and the brain. This is one of the reasons we lose focus and concentration during the day. The good news is that all you have to do to get the oxygen and blood flowing is to move. Even if you're in a job that requires you to be at a desk for long hours, you have the freedom to stand up every half hour and move your body right at your desk. You can set a timer to remind yourself to move throughout the day.

Chances are your sore, stiff shoulders and back may be all the reminder you need to remind yourself to move. Spend part of your desk time standing. If budget allows, consider a standing desk or a desk platform that moves up and down during the day. You might take it a step further and invest in a treadmill or bike desk.

The problem isn't just work, though. North Americans sit an average of eleven hours a day. It's hard to believe, but think about the amount of time you're sitting each day. You wake up and travel to work or school, usually sitting in a car, bus, or train. You get there and sit for hours, and have lunch, where you sit again. You sit the rest of the day, doing your work, and then sit on your way home.

You get home and sit down for dinner and then hit the phone, TV, or computer, all sitting. Then you go to bed. When do you move your body? You can do simple, everyday things to increase your movement, like walking around when you take personal phone calls, taking the stairs instead of the elevator, or stretching when you watch TV. If you're not moving, you already are or will eventually be overweight, sick, and weak.

GET MOVING

Moving every day is a good start to ending a sedentary lifestyle, but you'll still need to do at least twenty-five minutes of some type of physical activity three to five days a week. Select something you love to do that will build strength and flexibility while you move. I love yoga because it combines all three, plus I get a little meditation time on the mat.

Stretching exercises increase your flexibility and balance. In addition to making you less prone to tripping or falling, being flexible helps you prevent getting injured.

Stretching releases tension and stress, and can ease back, neck, or sciatic pain. In many cases you can avoid painkillers and surgery by doing the right stretches on a regular basis. Stretching keeps you limber mentally and physically and you can do it at your desk, while waiting in traffic or for a meeting, or while you watch TV. Plus it feels really good and doesn't require all that much effort. If you're into regular workouts, stretching will increase your range of motion and mobility.

Strength exercises include activities where you bear weight. This can be free weights, machines, or the resistance of your own body. Squats, lunges, push-ups, sit-ups, and pull-ups all count. Strength training exercises increase bone density, which helps to prevent broken bones when you fall. Another benefit is that they help you maintain a healthy body weight because you're burning body fat and increasing muscle. Your big plus is that you will feel more confident if you are more fit.

If you're intimidated by the thought of exercise, break it into manageable chunks. Try going on a ten-minute walk in the morning, playing three songs you love. It goes by quickly. Every hour at work, do one minute of movement. You can march in place, twist your body, lunges, whatever. One minute also goes by fast. Take another ten-minute walk when you get home, and make a phone call or listen to music. Without much effort, you get twenty-eight minutes of movement every day.

BRAIN AND BODY

Your physique definitely improves when you exercise and you look great, but the real benefits are things on the inside that you don't see. Getting your heart rate up for thirty minutes at a time, three to five days a week, does astonishing things for your brain and body. It might be difficult to get in the habit of a regular physical routine, but once you start, it becomes something you can't live without.

When you show up to take care of yourself, even if you're tired or don't feel like it, it's one of those small wins that help you achieve overall success in your life. Every time you do something new, you create new wiring in your brain that literally makes new neurological connections. The repetition of those actions over time conditions your body to learn how to do something without you having to think about it. This is how you form a habit.

Exercise is a habit that leads to a great mood, better energy, and a strong brain and body. In fact, it's the most transformative thing you can do for your brain. When you get more blood flow to the brain, you can help prevent or diminish symptoms in conditions like depression, Alzheimer's, and dementia. When you exercise, you're also pumping oxygen-rich blood to the lungs, which cleans out the arteries, which reduces your chance of stroke.

FEEL BETTER, SLEEP BETTER, LOOK BETTER

Exercise makes you feel better immediately, improves your mood overall, and improves your long-term memory. Immediately after you exercise, you're more alert and in a good mood because your brain and body release chemicals like endorphins, dopamine, and serotonin that make you feel good. The hippocampus and the prefrontal cortex are the parts of the brain most susceptible to cellular death, which causes disease and fuzzy thinking in old age. Exercise creates oxygen-rich blood that travels to the brain, creating neurogenesis (the creation of new cells) in the hippocampus, causing it to increase in size.

We use the hippocampus for long-term memory. Increasing blood flow to the hippocampus through exercise literally improves our memory function. The prefrontal cortex, the part of the brain responsible for decision-making and your personality, is also stimulated through exercise, putting you in a longer-term good mood.

Cardio exercise, the kind that makes you blood pump harder, oxygenates the blood, helping to prevent all of the lifestyle illnesses like type 2 diabetes, stroke, and cardiovascular disease. Cardio exercise also improves skin elasticity and delays signs of aging. Cardio could even enhance your sex life, as good blood flow leads to more arousal for women and less erectile dysfunction for men.

Are you having trouble sleeping? Exercise helps you fall asleep faster and stay asleep, as well as boosting your immune system and reducing your stress levels and anxiety.

So: when you exercise, you look better, you feel better, you sleep better, you act better, you perform better, and you have better sex. Is there any reason why you *wouldn't* want to get moving?

PLAYING VS. WORKING OUT

Maybe you think working out is boring or too hard, but exercise doesn't mean you have to wear special clothes and head to a gym or studio. It's also an opportunity to be outside and get social. Go for a walk or a hike, maybe with a friend, family member, or your pet. "Playtime" might sound a lot more enticing than "working" out.

If you're short on time, you can multitask exercise and play-time with your children by throwing or kicking a ball. If you need cardio, play tag with your kids, relatives, or your friends' kids. You'll create irreplaceable memories and get in shape.

If you're interested in meeting new people, it's a great idea to join a sports league like softball, kickball, tennis, or basketball. If you love to dance, turn up the music and move it, alone or with others. Go skating, ride a bike or a skateboard. Exercise is going to be a lot more appealing if it's something you love to do. Think of the physical things you loved to do as child, and start doing them again.

SWEAT OUT THE TOXINS

Detoxification is another way to stay healthy, and you don't even have to exercise to do it. There is one time when sitting can greatly improve your fitness level, and that's when you sit in a sauna or steam room. Sweating releases toxins from your body, and also helps with weight loss and cardiovascular health.

When you heat up the core body temperature in a sauna or steam room, your body produces more white blood cells, which help fight infection and viruses. Sitting in a sauna or steam room also helps to reduce inflammation, which causes joint and muscle pain. Sweating is a good and natural thing, so don't use antiperspirants. Underarm sweat is your body's way of releasing toxins, and that's probably why armpits smell bad. To combat odor, use nontoxic deodorant instead. I tap two fingers of baking soda on each underarm every day. It works like a charm.

HEAD FOR THE EXITS

Go outside and get some sun. It's the source of life on our planet, and our bodies thrive when the sun hits our skin. Direct exposure to sunlight helps our body to produce vitamin D, which enables our body to absorb calcium and phosphorus and facilitates normal immune system function. Sunlight kills bacteria and is great for skin conditions like psoriasis, acne, eczema, and other fungal infections. When the light from the sun penetrates our skin, it increases lymphocytes, which help build our immune system and defend the body against infections.

Sunshine also helps to cure depression and lower blood pressure. If you live in a climate where you can't get natural sunlight for a good portion of the year, consider a blue light, which provides some of the same benefits of natural sunlight. If you have access to natural sunlight, but you're sensitive to the sun, limit your exposure to the first two hours of the day and an hour before sunset. During these times, the sun is not as strong, but you will still gain the benefits of its light.

Good eye health is linked to being outdoors, if you put down your cell phone. When you're outside, your eyes have a chance to stop focusing on objects that are close, like screens and books, and look off into the distance. The human eye was designed to focus both near and far. Going outside allows our eyes to relax the focusing mechanism and go back to distance vision.

NATURAL ENERGY

Throughout history, humans have walked the Earth barefoot or in leather-soled shoes and slept on the ground, receiving the magnetic energy of the planet. The Earth's energy can create a stable internal bioelectric environment, helping to normalize all our body systems. This very well may be where the saying "stay grounded" originates.

It is believed that direct connection with the Earth can help lower inflammation in the body and fight free radicals. But now, when we do go outside, it's usually in thick rubber- or plastic-soled shoes that block the Earth's energy from entering our bodies as freely as it should. In addition to not receiving enough beneficial energy, we are blasted with radiation from cell phones, Wi-Fi, appliances, and microwaves, which all wreak havoc on tissues and cells, causing free radicals to stress our immune systems.

If you eat well, exercise, and detox and you still don't feel physically well, go outside. Stand, sit, or lie on the Earth. Go barefoot outside when you're in your yard, at a park, at the beach, or swimming in the ocean or a lake. If you want to benefit from the Earth's energy on a daily basis, buy leather-soled shoes and walk in them.

We all need to move, get outside, and create the habits that make these actions a part of our lives. We were given this incredible vessel, our body, to enjoy our journey through life. Just like any machine, it needs to be maintained. When it is neglected, it will fall into disrepair, preventing us from getting where we want to go.

If you're living a sedentary life that has made you sick, overweight, tired, or stressed, it's time to give yourself back your birthright: movement and being outside.

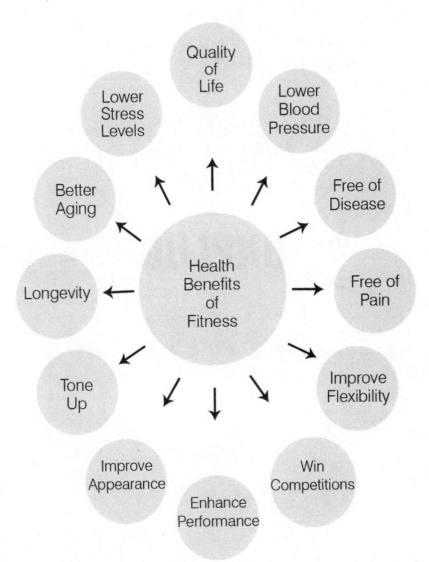

Almost everything
will work again
if you

UNPLUG

it for a few minutes,
including you.

- Anne Lamott

CHAPTER 11

Rejuvenation and Self-Care

Sleep is the most important way for the body to rejuvenate. Sleep refreshes and cleans the mind, and most people need about eight hours of it each night. How much sleep are you getting on average? What happens when you don't get enough?

PREVENTING DISEASE WITH SLEEP

When you get poor sleep or not enough of it over long periods of time, you put your life quality and health in jeopardy. When we sleep, our body has a chance to rebalance, regulate, regenerate cells, and process the experiences we've had in our environment. Getting good sleep is one of the main things we can do to help prevent lifestyle diseases and stay off prescribed medications, because sleep deprivation is linked to Alzheimer's, type 2 diabetes, cardiovascular disease, and stroke.

Sleep is when the brain has the opportunity to clean the waste that has accumulated inside of it all day. Because the brain is less preoccupied with tasks like thinking, moving, and eating, it can focus on flushing out the waste by shrinking the brain cells.

During sleep the brain secretes a fluid that rushes through and sucks up waste for elimination. The buildup of this waste, called amyloid plaque, is associated with Alzheimer's disease. The reason we feel "fuzzy" on the mornings we didn't get a good night's sleep might be because the brain didn't get to do a good job of taking out the garbage.

Do you tend to feel run-down when you don't sleep enough? That's because sleep also affects our immune system. You need adequate sleep to produce and release cytokine, a protein that regulates our immune system, which fights infection and inflammation.

SOUND SLEEPING

It's not just the quantity of sleep that matters for our mental and physical health; the quality of our sleep is equally important. There are two types of sleep we experience: light sleep (REM) and deep sleep.

When we are in light sleep, our brainwaves are similar to when we are awake. This is the time when we experience very vivid dreams, the ones we may remember upon waking. No one is 100 percent sure why we dream, but many believe it is the brain's way of processing all the things that have happened to us. In the light sleep state, the brain is still working hard on thinking.

Deep sleep is the kind of sleep we need for regeneration and recovery. When we are in deep sleep, the brain produces delta waves, or slow brain waves, which affect our ability to learn and the long-term memory areas of our brain. Getting deep sleep and experiencing delta waves is identified with the biological wellness that is more prevalent when we are young. As sleep quality is compromised by stress and environmental factors, the ability of our brains to produce the delta waves is diminished.

Understanding how to maintain deep sleep is imperative to maintaining a well-functioning brain and body.

CIRCADIAN RHYTHM

How does your environment affect the quality of sleep? There's something called your circadian rhythm that affects when you feel sleepy or awake, otherwise known as your sleep/wake cycle. The part of your brain that controls the sleep/wake cycle is the hypothalamus, and it's affected by darkness or light.

When it gets dark, your eyes send a signal to the hypothalamus that it's time to start getting ready to go to sleep. This causes your body to begin producing melatonin, which makes your body feel tired. Looking at your cellphone or laptop or watching TV before going to bed is contrary to your body's natural circadian rhythm, because the blue light those electronics emit sends waking signals to your body.

If you're having a hard time going to sleep at night, try turning off the electronics an hour before you go to sleep. If you like to read before bed, use a light with a yellow bulb, or "good night" bulb, which emits less of the blue light waves. In my house, all the lights are on dimmers. At 9 p.m., everything goes into "dim" mode, which I believe has been a factor that helps me sleep once I hit the pillow.

The wake cycle works with light when it's time to get up. Open the blinds so your eyes can see the sunlight and tell your brain to start the day. If you wake before the sun comes up or have alternative sleep/wake hours, turn the lights on to get your body moving in the wake cycle.

When you throw off your circadian rhythm by staying up late or waking up at different times, you may notice that you feel drowsy or less able to focus. The more consistent you can keep the sleep/wake cycle, the deeper and better sleep you'll likely experience.

Once you go to sleep, you want to stay asleep. See the following list for some helpful tips on getting the best night's sleep.

Mattress and Pillow

If you're having aches and pains when you wake up or restless nights, it might be your mattress or pillow. Try out different types of mattresses and pillows to see which works best with your body. A high-quality mattress is going to start at about $1,000, and it should last you about ten years. That winds up being twenty-seven cents a day to get a good night's sleep. Don't skimp on the mattress! Feeling well rested is worth a lot more than twenty-seven cents a day.

Blackout Curtains or Blinds

The darker the room is while you're sleeping, the deeper you will sleep. If you're a light or sensitive sleeper, even a small amount of light in your room could cause you to stay in REM sleep mode. There's a considerable amount of folklore around full moons and nutty human behavior. Today the full moon is the electric light outside your window, or the illumination from your cell phone. You will sleep better if you block the light.

Temperature

This really varies for everyone and can be difficult if there is someone else in the room who prefers a different temperature than you. If that's your situation, try the chiliPAD, a mattress pad the has the capability to be cool or hot, and splits the temperature on each side. If you're suffering from night sweats, your memory foam mattress makes you hot, you run hot, or it's just plain hot outside, you'll be able to get a cool night's sleep. You can also use individual duvets or covers for each person.

Sound

Using sound machines with white noise, sounds found in nature, or delta wave frequencies can help mask other distracting sounds that might interfere with staying asleep. If you're in a house where other people are awake when you're sleeping, a noisy city, or a hotel, sound machines can completely buffer the offensive noise and allow you to stay asleep.

Getting Up to Go to the Bathroom

We've been working on this one since we were toddlers. Make sure you go to the bathroom before you get into bed every night. If you have a sensitive bladder, stop drinking an hour or two before you go to sleep. Every single time I forget to do this, I wake up in the middle of the night.

Air Purifiers

Invisible particles from pollen, mold spores, smoke, pet dander, candles, pollution, and other irritants are floating around your bedroom. Using an air purifier can help to reduce or eliminate congestion, runny noses, dry mouth, allergies, asthma, and snoring.

The best one I've found for residential use is IQAir purifier. It also makes a white noise sound that blocks out other disturbing noise. I pump up the oxygen content in my room with a large snake plant. This is the body's time to rejuvenate; I make sure it's in a clean space.

Clear Your Mind

If you have a lot going on in your day, don't take it to bed with you. Try to do a mind dump before you hit the sheets by taking a bath, meditating, journaling, or talking to someone who cares. If your "to do" list wakes you up in the middle of the night, place a notebook and pen next to the bed with a small reading light. Write down what's on your mind and go back to bed. I try to do this without turning on a light.

Sleep Aids

Natural teas are really helpful. Kava from Yogi Tea is the one that works best for me. There's a key compound in the kava plant that triggers relaxation. When you drink it, you go out like a light and stay out, but you're not drowsy in the morning. CBD oil is also good for insomnia. I don't like it, but plenty of people swear by it.

Unplug

You blast yourself with plenty of cellular radiation all day. At night, give your body a fair chance to recuperate. Leave your phone in another room. If you use your phone to wake up, buy an alarm clock. You'll also be less likely to wake up in the middle of the night and check your messages and feeds. If you're worried about receiving an emergency call, don't worry; you'll hear the phone ring from the other room.

THE ART OF PAMPERING YOURSELF

Getting a good night's sleep is half the battle. You also need to pamper yourself. Start by telling yourself that self-care is a necessity, not a luxury. Taking time to relax and do things for you moves your brain from the fight-or-flight mode to the rest-and-digest mode. The act of loving yourself makes you feel emotionally better.

When you feel self-worth, you are able to tackle many more of the challenges you face in life. When you spend time doing things for just you, it's a temporary escape from what sometimes feels like a nonstop racetrack of existence. Pampering yourself once a week, or at least a few times a month, helps you to avoid feeling overwhelmed, burned out, or resentful. You'll not only feel better, but you'll look better too, which makes you more confident.

Bath Time

Instead of pushing through the sore back and neck or dull headache by popping Advil, try soaking in the tub with Epsom or magnesium salts, which allow your muscles to relax. Most people are lacking magnesium, a building block of life, so powerful that it helps plants convert sunlight to energy. Sitting in a tub of salts allows your skin to absorb it, eradicating inflammation in the body.

When you haven't had enough sleep, taking a bath is an excellent way to relax your body so that when you hit the sack, it's a deeper, more satisfying sleep. Being weightless in water is also a wonderful relief for your joints and bones. If you ever get a chance to go in natural bodies of water, stay in them for at least twenty minutes to absorb minerals that we don't get from our foods anymore.

Grooming

Take the time you need to groom yourself—that goes for men too. Deep condition your hair, do a face mask, breathe in essential oils, pumice your feet, moisturize dry skin, clean and cut nails and cuticles. You're going to feel great that you took care of YOU, and the bonus is that you will improve your appearance.

Massages

Get regular massages. If you can't afford expensive spa sessions, investigate massage schools or trade with a friend. I probably don't need to explain the incredible benefits of a massage. We all know massages relieve pain and stress, but they also help digestive disorders and problems with insomnia.

Meditation

We'll get more into meditation in a later chapter, but it belongs in this one too. Taking time to reflect, breathe, and be in a state of gratitude, even for a few minutes a day, improves your physiology and mood.

Hobbies

Listen to music you love and sing your heart out! Watch something funny and laugh until your stomach hurts! Or spend time on a hobby that is important to you. Whether you clean your guns, do a puzzle, make cookies, work on a car, play guitar, or sew a quilt, it doesn't matter. Spending time on the things that matter to you personally is a restorative act that brings balance back into your life.

We need to recharge emotionally and physically. We cannot routinely cheat ourselves of sleep and relaxation. Being exhausted makes dealing with the stressful situations we endure throughout the day so much more difficult. It leads to irrational behavior, fatigue, depression, anger, resentment, and apathy. You may be failing in the other parts of your life simply because you don't have the energy to deal with them. Good sleep and a little self-love releases stress and rejuvenates your body and soul.

TIPS FOR PRACTICING
Self-Care

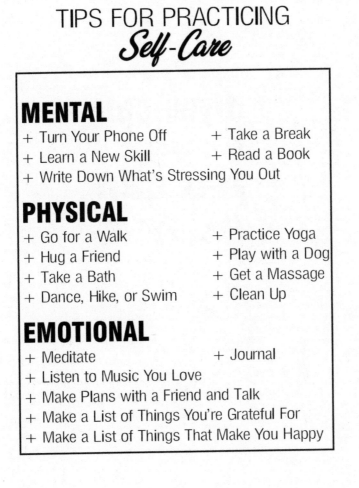

MENTAL
+ Turn Your Phone Off + Take a Break
+ Learn a New Skill   + Read a Book
+ Write Down What's Stressing You Out

PHYSICAL
+ Go for a Walk   + Practice Yoga
+ Hug a Friend   + Play with a Dog
+ Take a Bath   + Get a Massage
+ Dance, Hike, or Swim + Clean Up

EMOTIONAL
+ Meditate   + Journal
+ Listen to Music You Love
+ Make Plans with a Friend and Talk
+ Make a List of Things You're Grateful For
+ Make a List of Things That Make You Happy

If you can *change your mind,* **you can** *change your life.*

- Author Unknown

CHAPTER 12

Stress

When we hear the word *stress*, we immediately associate bad feelings with it. It's not all bad, though. Stress is a completely normal human reaction that allows us to function in times of uncertainty or danger.

A small burst of short-term stress gives us the extra push of urgency we need to complete something important, like slamming the brakes of a car, or lifting something heavy when a life is in jeopardy, or running fast from danger.

Your body is also in a stress state when you try to convince someone to agree with you, when you engage in a challenging physical activity like a dance competition, or when you have an orgasm. So clearly, we don't want to avoid stress completely.

NEGATIVE STRESS

Stress becomes a problem when we endure it for long periods of time. Instead of being able to see through to the end of our issue, we become overtaken with feelings of dread, anxiety, anger, loneliness, frustration, and sadness. These feelings give us the impression that we are powerless and have no control. Being under this type of stress long term is taxing to our body's systems, contributing to fatigue, insomnia, and even a shorter life.

Living in a stressed state negatively affects our ability to perform socially, physically, and intellectually. Learning how to manage stress is critical to maintaining equilibrium in all of our quadrants. Conversely, the more able we are to master each quadrant, the less likely we are to experience states of chronic stress.

THE PHYSIOLOGY OF STRESS

What happens to our body when we experience stress? Our nervous system operates in two modes: sympathetic, which prepares it for fight or flight; and parasympathetic, when the body rests and digests.

When we experience any type of stress, the body uses the sympathetic nervous system to incite action. Biochemical reactions temporarily take over, and any system that is not needed for our immediate survival is slowed down or stopped. Cortisol and adrenaline are created and start to flow. Our eyes dilate, while our blood vessels constrict. Our muscles tremble and tense up. Sweating or chills may occur. Breathing becomes shallow or quick. The heart starts to beat faster to pump harder so it can get oxygen to the brain. The stomach stops making digestive enzymes, which causes you to burn glucose instead of fat.

When all of these biochemical reactions happen, your brain gets what's called "tunnel vision." This enables the brain to focus mostly on the task at hand. These reactions are the body's way of preparing to defend itself or get the heck out of the way. Once the perceived or real danger has subsided, your body has the chance to return to its resting state.

In modern society, we tend to live in prolonged and sometimes constant states of heightened stress, causing our bodies to stay in the stressed condition. Over time this can cause our immune system to become compromised, paving the way for frequent colds, aches, and pains. Weight gain and digestion issues, like diarrhea or constipation, are also common side effects of stress because the digestive system stops working efficiently.

Stress often affects sleep, keeping you awake at night. Chronic sleep deprivation can lead to memory problems, anxiety, even depression. If depression sets in, you could find yourself losing your sex drive, neglecting your responsibilities, and withdrawing from people. Stress can even lead to premature death.

CHANGING OUR PERCEPTION

In her book, *The Telomere Effect: A Revolutionary Approach to Living Younger, Healthier, Longer,* Nobel Prize–winner Elizabeth Blackburn discuss her studies about how the length of our telomeres is directly related to how long we will live. She explains how chronic stress shortens our telomeres and our lives.

Chromosomes, which carry our genetic material, have telomeres at the ends of them. Every human starts life as a single cell that eventually multiplies into 200 billion cells. Every time a new cell is formed, it is an exact copy of that person's DNA. Each time a "copy" of a cell is made, it has a shorter telomere on the end of it.

Eventually the telomeres get so short, or damaged, that the cell dies because it thinks the DNA is being compromised. This is how we age. Telomeres depend on a chemical called telomerase to thrive. As we age, telomerase production slows down as the telomeres shorten.

We start to show the signs of aging like wrinkles from skin cell death, and are subject to increased illness from immune cell death. Similarly, when people are under enormous amounts of stress for long periods of time, their telomerase production is reduced, causing the telomeres to disintegrate faster. The more stress a person perceives him- or herself to be in, the faster the disintegration.

However, when people viewed stressful situations as challenges that could be met, the negative effect on their bodies was much less. Dr. Blackburn's studies show that what and how you think about stress matters, because it has a profound effect on how the body functions. The evidence points to the fact that too much stress is literally life-threatening.

The good news is that if you handle stress better, eat properly, get moderate exercise, chill out, and look on the bright side in your life, you can reverse the damage, lengthen the telomeres, and extend your life, or at least the healthy part of your life. Are you starting to see how all the quadrants affect each other, and why we must have balance in each of them?

CELL STRESS

Why are we so stressed? Potential stressors are everywhere and too many things are being considered urgent, rather than where they belong in the spectrum of priority. Technology has created expectations for immediacy that human beings are not wired to fulfill.

Just because we have a cell phone, we are expected to answer texts and calls immediately. People become irritable when we don't. Often I see others stop having a face-to-face conversation with someone to return a text or pick up the call of someone else.

Feeling the need to immediately respond to a call or text is one of the many ways we are being pulled into too many directions. It's also rude to stop a conversation with someone to respond to someone else. If it's not a true emergency, the person in front of your face or the one already on the call with you has priority.

If possible, try leaving the phone off during some of your free time. At least start with not taking it to the bathroom or looking at it when you stop at a traffic light. Give yourself a few minutes to look around at your environment and take a breath. Look up at the sky and zone out for a few seconds to decompress instead of grabbing your phone and frantically searching for something to occupy your time.

BEING TOO AVAILABLE

Addiction to the cell phone is the reason so many people feel they don't have enough time. There's always something "to do" on the phone. But for some, actual work or social duties never end because they allow themselves to be reached 24/7 by email, phone, or text. These people really have no time because these demands steal their personal time.

It's unsustainable and overly stressful to be so available. We find it hard to say no and create boundaries, but we must. Some people suffer from FOMO, fear of missing out. They accept every invitation to every opportunity. This stress you might feel from being overbooked is very real, but it's also self-imposed. Learn how to let some go.

Anyone have that friend or family member who never stops asking for favors? Learn how to say "I am not available." Any of you have clients who think it's reasonable to call you on Saturday morning or at 9:30 at night because that's when they are free? Don't pick up those calls.

When I first met my husband, I used to pick up my design clients' calls late into the night and on the weekends. He looked at me one day and said, "Enough. You run a business, and you answer the phone during business hours. There's no such thing as a true interior design emergency. It can wait."

And you know what? He was right. Taking his advice gave me back my nights and weekends. I'm sure you can imagine how much the decision to not always be available has reduced my stress.

If you feel like this is something that could lower your stress, give it a try. And If you're thinking *there's no way I could do that*, you may want to go back and read chapters 6 and 7 on Meaningful Work and Changing Careers. This is your life; remember that you are in charge of your own happiness. Set boundaries.

POTENTIAL STRESSORS

We all face stressors in our lives, some more trying than others. What type of stress are you experiencing in your life?

- Death of a loved one
- Moving
- New job
- Getting fired
- Remodeling a house
- Divorce
- Illness
- Work
- School
- Relationship problems
- Finances
- Kids—having them and not being able to have them
- Social injustice
- Getting dumped
- Not getting your way
- Losing something valuable

- Your commute
- A jerk
- Dealing with your internet provider
- Taxes
- Whatever else bothers you

These things are going to happen; there's no way to avoid them.

How are you dealing with them? Are you making yourself sick? Acting out against people you love? Substance abuse? Totally giving up hope? You've probably realized by now that unconstructive actions and feelings make the initial stress even more intense.

Doing something mean or stupid makes us feel guilty on top of feeling out of control. When you react positively to the stress, it does not have to be harmful to your body or your life. When you are able to take mental control over your situation and tell yourself "this too shall pass," your body is able to leave the sympathetic nervous system response and return to the parasympathetic state. In this more relaxed state, all systems are firing, so you feel well and are able to deal with your problem.

Staying calm in the face of a challenge, instead of freaking out, allows your brain to think rationally. The act of just paying attention to physical stress symptoms like the racing heart, the tightened muscles, the beads of sweat, and being able to realize that your body is just doing its job, puts you back into a feeling of control. Even though the conditions you're dealing with may be extremely difficult, believing you will prevail can actually prime your brain and body to succeed.

MAKING LESS STRESS

You can also take proactive measures to reduce small daily stressors so you are more capable of handling others that come your way. How many of you lose your keys, glasses, or wallet frequently? How much stress do you feel when you're already cutting it close on time and you wind up being late and frustrated because you have to search the house for twenty minutes to find something? Put these items in one place when you enter the house and your problem is solved. Now you know where things will be, and this particular stress is gone.

How many routine, simple areas can you take steps in to eliminate stress? Would tidying up so you can find what you're looking for make your life less stressful? How about filling your car with gas the night before you have to go somewhere in case you need more time in the morning?

The physiological things you're feeling in your body may actually make you crave connections with other people. Stress could have the benefits of making you more compassionate about the difficulty of others, and long to share how you feel. Alongside the cortisol and adrenaline hormones that are released when you are stressed, there is the hormone oxytocin. Oxytocin makes us want to be close to others and motivates us to seek support from people who love us.

Instead of keeping your feelings to yourself when you feel stressed out, talk to someone who cares about you, and get a hug. It will release even more oxytocin, which will make you feel better. It's not a coincidence that our bodies release a hormone that makes connection desirable. It's our bodies' built-in navigation tool that leads us to a source of comfort that can, in turn, lower our stress.

Taking care of yourself by sleeping enough, eating nutrient-rich foods, relaxing, exercising, and meditating, which we explore in a later chapter, are remarkable advantages for stress reduction and the capacity to handle stress. Sometimes all you need to do is think positive thoughts and breathe to move through challenges.

In chapter 6 we learned about meaningful work. When your workload is stressful, having a deeper sense of meaning behind the demands helps to alleviate destructive feelings of being overwhelmed. When you're working on something that you care about, the tasks don't seem as mundane, pointless, and overpowering. If too many things are being thrown at you to handle, consider how to break them down into manageable portions and communicate to others how they can realistically be delivered. Enforce reasonable boundaries.

IMMEDIATE STRESS-REDUCTION TECHNIQUE

I learned a breathing technique from yoga teacher Brenda Strong that is very effective for calming down in a moment of anxiety. It's called the ujjayi breath. You breathe in a long deep breath through the nose and breathe out of the mouth, saying "HA."

Breathe in again and close your mouth halfway, feeling the HA sound in the back of your throat, the HA sounding more like a whisper. Inhale through the nose; exhale through the mouth with your eyes closed—whisper HA. Relax your face, jaw, chest, and hips, all the way to your feet. Do this for one minute, or as long as you need, to stop the fight-or-flight symptoms, and move your body back to rest-and-digest mode.

When I do this, I think of breathing in the cool blue air (relax) and breathing out the red-hot air (stress). It helps me visualize the positive energy entering and the stress leaving my body.

Stress can be greatly reduced by saying no, creating boundaries, and reaching out to your social connections. Viewing stress as a challenge to be resolved, instead of an insurmountable problem, will help to alleviate harmful psychological and physical effects. The stressors we encounter in our lives are not going away. The way we choose to deal with them makes all the difference in how stress affects us.

Sometimes you're going to lose it. You're going to break or blow. Stress is going to momentarily get the best of you. It happens to us all, and that's OK. Stop. Breathe. Start thinking of how to move forward. You can and you will.

HOW STRESS AFFECTS YOU

MIND

Trouble Thinking Clearly
Inability to Concentrate
Memory Problems
Poor Judgment
Indecisiveness
Fearfulness
Negativity
Worrying

BODY

Muscle Tension, Stiffness
Headaches / Backaches
Diarrhea / Constipation
Weight Gain / Loss
Loss of Sex Drive
Rapid Heartbeat
Frequent Colds
Fibromyalgia
Insomnia

EMOTIONS

Apathy
Agitation
Depression
Restlessness
Short Temper
Feeling Tense & Irritable

BEHAVIOR

Jaw Clenching
Teeth Grinding
Isolating Yourself
Eating More/Less
Sleeping Too Little
Sleeping Too Much
Overdoing Activities
Using Alcohol/Drugs
to Decompress

PART IV
SPIRITUALITY

MEDITATION
is like a gym
in which
you develop
the powerful

mental muscles

of
calm and insight.

- Ajahn Brahm

CHAPTER 13

Meditation

Meditation or mindfulness is a simple mental technique used to gain an aware state for the purpose of quieting the mind and gaining better control of our behavior. Many people confuse meditation with religion or being hypnotized. The word *meditation* brings up cultlike images of hippies or secluded monks. While these people do often meditate, the practice is not exclusive to their domains.

Meditation works for anyone, from any culture. Meditation techniques allow you to take attention away from your incessant thoughts and emotions, the "monkey mind," so that you can tune in to a clearer state of being. Similar to the way dreaming helps our mind to make sense of the day's events, meditation helps our brain to sort outside influences by making the brain's hemispheres work together. When this happens, a person is able to become more proactive and less reactive to external situations.

MAINSTREAM MEDITATION

If you think about how many people have short attention spans, lack of focus, or frequent overreactions like inappropriate anger, you start to understand the effect that meditation could have on an entire society. Imagine what the world would be like if people had better control over their reactions. When people are calm and thoughtful instead of stressed and impulsive, humanity will thrive.

We're starting hear a lot about meditation and mindfulness in the mainstream, and it's becoming associated with well-respected, high-profile people as contributing to their successes. I was pleasantly surprised when I learned my daughter's school had started to teach mindfulness classes. It's an incredible gift to give children the power to begin controlling their emotions and behavior at the beginning of their lives.

Meditation also has the added benefit of putting the ego in check as the focus goes away from "me" to feeling a connection to the universe and all things. When you feel connected to others on a spiritual level, you gain the ability to be compassionate. Your level of appreciation expands when you concentrate on gratitude instead of expectations.

NOT FEELING IT?

If practicing mindfulness can be life changing, why are so many people resistant to trying it? What could be better than learning how to harness the power to transform your life for the better? What's stopping you?

Do you think it's too boring to sit and think about nothing? It's definitely strange to sit unplugged for a period of time, all alone, and try to think about nothing. I can see how that description of meditation would compare to watching paint dry on a wall. But when you engage in a regular meditation practice, you actually look forward to when you can have that private, quiet time.

How about those of you who can't sit still? Did you know that you could lie down or even walk while you meditate? And once you learn how to quiet your mind, you also learn how to sit still and let it flow.

You may feel like a meditation practice is too time consuming. It doesn't have to be. You can get the same benefits from a few minutes a day of meditation as you do from a longer practice.

Maybe you tried in the past, and your mind was all over the place, so you quit. That's exactly why people meditate, to help stop the mind from racing. If you continue to practice, you will eventually get to that place.

You might think meditating is for weirdos. It's not something serious people do. But I bet I could name someone you admire who practices meditation.

I completely understand all of these reasons for avoiding meditation, because I felt the exact same way for a very long time. In fact, it took me fifteen years to get the hang of meditation.

It wasn't a straight shot, though. Every few years I would try a different variety for a few sessions before I would eventually quit. Because I hadn't found the right method, I kept dismissing the practice as unnecessary, boring, and a waste of my time. In the back of my mind, I knew I was telling myself a story because I was frustrated that I hadn't "figured it out."

As I read more books by and about people that I admired, I realized that there was a glaring commonality among them: they all practiced a form of meditation. Even more interesting was that the people I looked up to the most actually said that they credited their practice of meditation for their prosperity and happiness.

A few A-listers I knew personally told me that they woke up and went to bed reciting "grateful" meditations. That seemed easy enough; I felt very grateful for lots of things. So I started walking around telling the Universe how grateful I was, out loud, sometimes when others were present. "Thank you, Universe, for this delicious sweet orange. Thank you, Universe, for the invigorating yoga class."

It made my daughter and her friends giggle when I said these verbal meditations of gratitude, but it was really making a difference in my life and making me feel grounded and happy. Then I listened to a Tim Ferriss podcast with Tony Robbins, who spoke about how he spends nine minutes a day in meditation: three minutes being grateful, three minutes clearing his mind and connecting to the Universe, and three minutes on what will impact his day. I had an epiphany!

The reason I didn't like meditating was because I was trying to think about nothing for thirty minutes, and that didn't resonate with me mentally or physically. Here was this world-class guru who said he felt the same way. I modified my meditation practice to something that worked for me, and now it's something I would never do without.

MEDICAL BENEFITS

If you haven't figured it out by now, I'm all about the science and how things actually affect our bodies and brains. Meditation is no exception. When you practice meditation, you can change your brain structure. That's because whenever you engage in a behavior over and over again, it leads to changes in your brain's neuroplasticity and how the neurons communicate with each other.

Put more simply, when you meditate, you rewire the brain and you can also grow your brain. The front part of the brain controls problem solving, emotional expression, memory, empathy, and judgment. As we get older, it's normal for this part of the brain to shrink, which is why some become more irritable and confused as they age.

Participants who practiced meditation in an eight-week study at Harvard, led by Sara Lazar, were tested with MRI machines that showed that areas of the brain, including the frontal cortex, increased in size. The thickening of the prefrontal cortex, which controls creativity and attention span, occurred as a result of a consistent meditation practice. The hippocampus, regulating memory and emotions, increased with meditation.

An area of the brain responsible for empathy and compassion, called the temporoparietal junction, also increased in people who meditated. Interestingly, the amygdala, the part of the brain in control of stress reaction, decreased in the meditators. By training the mind to be calm and less stressed through meditation techniques, you biochemically enable it to perform in a heightened state.

MORE BENEFITS

In addition to a bigger brain, meditation has many other "feel-good" long-term benefits.

Reduce Stress

Being able to remain calm when responding to your environment gives you the feeling of control and reduces physiological symptoms of stress, like high blood pressure and lower immunity.

Control Anxiety

Meditation enables you to stop the brain chatter and negative and obsessive thoughts and focus on the positive.

Reduce Depression

Daily meditation has been shown to reduce the release of cytokine chemicals in your brain. Cytokines have a negative effect on your mood, making it difficult to have a positive outlook.

Self-Awareness

Meditation helps you to reflect on your thoughts and actions. Often, we're focusing on other things and moving too quickly through our day to understand what is causing mental anguish or drama.

When you give yourself space to ponder the way you behave, you are able to identify the base feelings causing the reactive behavior, and reroute.

Being in meditation also encourages you to pay attention to your inner voice and trust your gut.

Increase Attention Span

Throughout our days, we're pulled in so many directions. Learning how to slow down and direct your mind to one thought carries through to how you handle your tasks and activities. You also become more able to connect with others and truly listen and be present in conversations. This is one of the most important skills for a successful relationship.

Mental Discipline

Learning how to stay present and examine how we respond to internal and external triggers sets us up to be able to break harmful habits, like addiction, bad relationships, and self-loathing.

Happier

Being grateful and focusing on abundance, rather than absence, allows you to recognize what you have, rather than what you're missing. You can literally find yourself smiling when you think of the things that you feel gratitude for, no matter how small. Gaining control of your emotions and actions makes you nicer and more compassionate toward others, which results in being happier.

Insomnia

Once you learn how to turn off the chatter in your brain, you can fall asleep. When you wake up in the middle of the night thinking about what happened or what's coming, you are able to stop thinking, breathe, and go back to sleep. If I ever find myself awake in the middle of the night starting to think, I tell myself, "Now is not the time for this, go to sleep." It works and it's directly because of my meditation practice. Being able to sleep a sound and full night is priceless.

Better Sex

Being stressed out increases cortisol and adrenaline hormones in the body, which decreases sex drive. In women, increased levels of these hormones could inhibit the ability to have an orgasm. When you decrease stress through meditation, you lower the cortisol and adrenaline levels, so physically, you're more relaxed and ready for action.

More importantly, knowing how to turn on thoughts from the past and understanding what you need to do in the future allows you to be present in the now. When you can focus on the pleasure of the moment, you're probably going to enjoy it a lot more.

Controlling Pain

Harvard studies have shown that pain involves both the mind and the body. People suffering from chronic pain have been able to reduce their perception of the pain through meditation, thereby feeling like they have less pain. Alternatively, when you have rewired your brain to feel like it is always in pain, you might still experience pain even when there are no physical symptoms.

If you can grow the brain with meditation, you can surely help alleviate the perception of physical pain with it.

TYPES OF MEDITATION

How do you meditate? The goal in meditation is become aware of the power in your mind, body, and breath. Find your spot, preferably a quiet one. Start by taking a few deep breaths to get your central nervous system into the parasympathetic state by thinking, *I am relaxed and I can do this.*

If you're going for stationary meditation, sit or lie down in a comfortable position with your eyes open or closed. Start to focus on your body, how you feel, and your breath. If your mind starts wandering to other thoughts, just notice that and come back to what you were focusing on or pay attention to the breath going in and out of your abdomen and chest.

Don't fight with the thoughts that come up; just let them pass. There's no right amount of time or one style of meditation. You can try different amounts of time and different types of meditation until you figure out what resonates with you.

There are dozens of recognized meditation techniques. To learn about the various forms, search Google for "33 types of meditation explained simply for beginners." Below, there are brief descriptions of the most popular types of meditation and their benefits. When it comes to meditation, there's definitely something for everyone.

My morning routine combines a few styles, and I spend about ten minutes in meditation each day. If you spot something that looks interesting, dive deeper and research it more on Google or YouTube.

Kundalini

This one is very physical. You sit with crossed legs and use the "breath of fire" and pump your arms to unleash the energy inside of you, releasing creativity, sexual energy, emotional balance, and vitality. I start my meditation with this powerful breath to get my blood moving and my mind ready to go to a new place.

Mindfulness

This is a very low-energy meditation where you keep your eyes closed, think about what you are thankful for, and let thoughts pass through. I do this for the first third of my practice.

Primordial Sound, Mantra, or Transcendental

These are some of the most popular types of meditation in Western culture. They involve repeating a mantra over and over. I tried this unsuccessfully. I felt ridiculous repeating the same thing over and over for thirty minutes. It's OK if you feel that way about any of these practices. There are so many—something will click for you.

Pranayama

Focus on the breath going in and out of the nostrils. A lot of yoga classes do this at the beginning. It's supposed to reduce anxiety. It actually makes me anxious.

Walking Meditation

If sitting or lying down isn't your jam, try a walking meditation. This can be done by walking in any natural environment, taking deep breaths, and appreciating your surroundings. If you do this when you walk, jog, or hike, you may already be meditating without even knowing it. You can also do this one as a passenger on a drive by looking out the window.

Tonglen

Breathe in suffering and exhale compassion. This is great if you are dealing with a challenging person. Apparently blessing or sending good vibes to something you don't like makes it less awful to you. Sounds reasonable.

Vipassana

If you're experiencing jealousy, this practice teaches you to accept things the way they are, purifying the mind of hatred, greed, and delusion. Too bad we didn't know about this one back in high school!

Loving Thoughtfulness

Repeat loving phrases that make you feel happy. You direct these thoughts to people who make you feel angry.

Trataka or Sungazing

Focus your eyes on one point. An additional benefit is if you look at something far away, like the sun. It's supposed to strengthen your eyes. I love this one when I really need a kick of energy or confidence. *Important safety tip:* If you're going to look at the sun, do it ten minutes after sunrise or twenty minutes before sunset.

Yoga Nidra or Body Scan

This meditation includes focusing on every single part of the body down to the fingertips. Start anywhere and move around, like fingertips to the palms, to the wrists, to the elbows, etc., sending relaxation all over your body. If you wake up in the middle of the night and can't fall back asleep, try bringing this focused awareness to your mind. You'll likely fall back asleep before you finish.

Grounding

Standing barefoot or sitting on the Earth, aligning the body with the Earth's energy. It makes you feel calm, in control, refreshed, and full of peace.

Sound Bath or Gong

This is when you listen to the sounds of crystal bowls or gongs that ring in complementary frequencies to your body. It's like getting a piano tuning for your cells.

Guided

A voice guides you step by step through your experience. This is really good if you're stuck with all the other methods or don't know how to start. Check out guided meditation on YouTube and find a voice, style, and amount of time that you like.

Merkaba

This one involves energetic fields and is fairly complex, involving sacred polyhedrons. The goal is to help one achieve a higher state of consciousness and become aware of several fields of energy that surround us. After I finish writing this book, I'm going to study this practice.

Religion

Some people consider their faith and willingness to surrender to their God as a form of meditation.

––––––––––––

Which one sounds like you? Try one and see how it makes you feel. The key to making mental and physical changes through meditation is to practice every day.

If you can't make it one day, do not stress out about it. Pick it back up the very next day. You don't want meditation to feel like another chore, or something you failed to do.

Anyone can reduce stress and change their brain structure by meditating each day. Learning and mastering the skills of meditation will change your relationships, finances, and health if you do the work. It may empower you to live your fullest life. It has for me.

Spirituality

- The experience of a higher being or force greater than ourselves
- Helps us to find meaning and purpose in the things we value
- A sense that there is more to life than material things
- The search for meaning in life events
- Can bring hope and meaning at times of suffering and loss
- Something everyone can experience
- Yearning for connection to the universe
- A quality that goes beyond religion, and strives for inspiration

**Your life
is controlled
by what you
focus on.**

-Tony Robbins

CHAPTER 14

Law of Attraction

The law of attraction is the belief that you will attract positive or negative events, people, and things into your life simply by thinking about them. The metaphysical principle behind this is that we create our own reality based on what we think. When we put out expectations for something, it inevitably affects the outcome.

Some people consider this law to be one of the most powerful forces in the Universe. They use techniques of positive thinking, affirmations, and visualization to attract the things they want. Instead of concentrating on the things you don't want, you put all of your attention on the things you would like to happen and ask the Universe to send them to you.

HOW THE MAGIC WORKS

The act of consciously knowing and thinking about what you want already propels you toward achieving it. This is done with the power of your imagination and its ability to manifest awesome and different things, rather than what we've already seen.

If that's confusing, think about great inventors who created things, like Albert Einstein or Steve Jobs. These theories and products were not in existence prior to being imagined and then realized. By using thoughts and visualization to see the world as how they expected it to be, they were able to create a new reality for everyone on the planet.

Everything you see came into existence from something that wasn't previously there. At one time in the past there was no spaghetti, movies, or furniture. Someone called these things into being what they are today by the power of manifestation. You have the same ability to use your intentions to create your own reality as well.

LIKE ATTRACTS LIKE

You are like a magnet, and you will attract what you think about because your thoughts influence your behavior and actions and make you become who you are. If you're unhappy with who you are, you must change what you think about. If you're a confident thinker, and you believe good things will happen to you, you will walk through life with an air of confidence. People are attracted to that.

When you see a place for yourself at the table of life, you will behave like you deserve to be at the table and make yourself willing to receive the invitation. What you put out comes right back to you. Thinking, feeling, and being positive will open new doors and create new opportunities that didn't exist for you in the past. This is the law of attraction.

When you are positive and good things are happening to you, you gain courage that enables you to push through self-doubt and other roadblocks to your success. On the flip side, if you are a negative thinker, pessimistic or overly skeptical, that's exactly how you will behave. What do you think you will attract by behaving that way?

THE POWER OF YOUR THOUGHTS

So how do we tap into this kind of energy and use positive thoughts to create a life that we love? The law of attraction works by refocusing our attention on new behaviors, new thoughts, new actions, and new emotions instead of being stuck in the past. What you constantly think about is what you will make happen.

We have nearly 700,000 thoughts a day, and almost all of those thoughts are the same thoughts we had yesterday. If you consistently focus only on what is from the past, you are unable to change anything in your life. If your experiences and thoughts are all positive, then that's a great thing.

Unfortunately, most people walk around with thoughts of fear, loss, being inferior, not believing they can succeed, not knowing what they want, and remembering their failures or limits. You have got to monitor your thoughts and stop thinking this way. Doing so forms expectations that negative things will happen to you and you will act accordingly, attracting the undesirable. Your personality is a result of the way you act and how you feel, and this becomes your reality.

When you are able to change these things, you can change your personality and your future. What are your first thoughts when you wake up? Are you dreading the day ahead and thinking about the problems you need to deal with? Or do you wake up with grateful thoughts for what you have, and how the day will be filled with opportunity?

YOUR WORDS

What are your conversations about? Are they filled with gossip and bad-mouthing of other people? Do you make excuses for yourself and your situation by blaming others? Are you envious of people who have things you that want, and do you talk badly about them in an attempt to feel better about yourself?

What is your language like? Is it full of *yes, I can, that's possible*? Or is it full of *no, I don't, I can't, I'm not*? Can you imagine how these two different ways of speaking affect others' behavior toward you?

Do you spend your energy focusing on why things keep happening to you? How do you imagine things could be if you changed those thoughts and your language? What if your conversations changed to productive words about how you're going to accomplish your goals?

Think about the look on your face when you are thinking about something bad, or unfair, or difficult. It's a look of despair or unhappiness. Now think about the look on your face when you just did something really well, or got incredible news, or made someone else happy. You might have even smiled when you had those thoughts. I just did.

What kinds of vibes or energy are you throwing out into the world? And who will be attracted to it? That's the law of attraction in its most basic form.

FOCUSING ON WHAT WE WANT, NOT WHAT ALREADY HAPPENED

We move through our lives being affected by our experiences. How is your external environment guiding how you think, feel, and act? We all do mostly the same things each day. We see the same people, we listen to the same radio and TV personalities, and we think the same thoughts. There's an overwhelming amount of negativity that we absorb.

If the same unconstructive information is playing in our brains over and over again, how can we ever expect to have a different outcome? This is where our imagination and meditation come into play. When you stop concentrating on the past and the known and replace it with something greater, you disassociate your thoughts, feelings, and actions from the old ways.

By thinking new thoughts of possibility, love, and joy, you gain the power to change your life. Thinking these types of thoughts activates new wiring and changes the biochemistry of your brain. This creates new memories and feelings that help to change the outcome of your future. If you continue to think these new thoughts, you will start acting differently.

Some people think the law of attraction is nonsense because they refuse to believe that just thinking about something could cause a desired effect. I completely agree. Thinking without action won't amount to much.

You cannot just sit on your meditation pillow, thinking a five-million-dollar check will magically arrive in your mailbox, and then it does. You'd have to take some kind of action for that to happen, like creating a business or writing a song. The thinking part is preparing your entire focus on a goal and then setting yourself up to take actions to achieve that goal.

The magic happens when you know what you want and believe intensely that you are going to be it or get it. These beliefs thrust you past your fears and put you in the mindset to do what it takes to make your dreams come true. That's the secret, and it all starts with your thoughts.

When you start to think of abundance and that you are worthy, instead of thinking you are in need and worthless, you will start to feel those things. Feeling these things enables you to be these things. Now, instead of being affected by the routines you do each day, you're able to create new pathways and rewrite your reality.

ASK, BELIEVE, RECEIVE

These three catchy and succinct words are the entire formula to change the way you think, change your behavior, and manifest your destiny. I think the hardest thing for most people is to ask. They either feel guilty for wanting something for themselves or have never given themselves permission to really think about what would truly make them happy.

In order to ask, you must be clear about what you want to create. You need to make a choice to decide what it is going to be and how it is going to be. You must realize what you want to be or what you want to have before you will ever become that person and have that life.

Knowing what you want is sometimes the most difficult part. We're so busy in our daily lives that we don't devote time to this kind of deep thought. You can practice this when you meditate. Think about your clear vision, and ask the Universe to give it to you. You can ask out loud or quietly in your mind.

Next, you must believe. To believe you will become or have something else, something greater than what you are, you must face the truth of what it takes to become that thing. You must look at that pro athlete, CEO, or singer and see what it takes to accomplish what they've accomplished and be willing to go on that journey.

I love this quote from author Bob Proctor: "If you can see it in your mind, you can hold it in your hand." When you believe that you have something, you start to feel like what it's like to have it. When you meditate on this thing, think about its attributes. What does it look like, feel like, taste like, smell like? Some people find it very useful to make vision boards or visual cues so they can focus on what they want every time they look at it. You can also just close your eyes and see it.

Finally, you receive. You think as if that thing you want has already happened. If what you want is to get married to a wonderful spouse and have a family, think thoughts of the way the person looks at you, the way they make you feel. Imagine big celebrations with your family all around you, giving you kisses and hugs.

Envision waking up next to this person, or going on a vacation to the beach, holding hands while walking along the shoreline together. See the smiles on the faces of your children while they play in the sand. Sensory visualization is how you manifest the things you want. Love yourself and believe that these things are happening for you, whatever they are. Move past your fears of not being able to get these things and fake it till you make it.

ATTRACTING TRUE LOVE

I know this power works because I manifested the life I now have by asking for, believing in, and receiving my lifelong dream of having a family of my own. At thirty-six, I was still single and starting to get a little bit nervous about my dream coming true. It was time for serious focus.

I placed a magazine picture of a happy couple on my bedroom wall. The man in the picture had the physical attributes of someone I wanted to look at forever. The lady looked a bit like me. They were well dressed and drinking champagne, implying their financial well-being in addition to their celebratory nature. Every single morning and night for two months I said, "Hello, husband," and blew him a kiss.

Then, after two years of dating online, just when I was going to let my subscription expire, a smile came across my screen. I knew immediately that this was my guy. He even looked like the man on my wall. After a week of nonstop calls and texts, we met in person. He showed up at my door with a bottle of champagne. That, my friends, is the power of attraction.

Now I have two pictures on my wall. One picture is of an older man and two generations of girls, his daughter and granddaughter, sitting in a beautiful kitchen. There's another one with two grandparents, a daughter, her husband, and two grandchildren walking together on a gorgeous beach. Check back in with me in twenty years—I bet you anything these magazine photos will match ones taken of my family.

Also posted on my wall above my desk is a check written out to myself for $3,000,000. That's what I'd like to make in my construction and design businesses this year. Actor Jim Carrey wrote a big check to himself at the beginning of his career and credits it for being part of his enormous success. If it worked for him, why not you or me? But don't forget: you gotta show up and do the work!

GRATITUDE, PATIENCE, AND PERSISTENCE

Practice gratitude for what you already have in your life and think about how you have attracted other good things in your life. Keep performing the actions that are leading you in the right direction and stop doing the things that are leading you away from your goals. When you start thinking negative thoughts about how you can't do it, stop. Go back to believing and receiving. Throughout your days, focus on these positive thoughts.

When challenging things happen in your life, ask yourself why. *What is this moment supposed to teach me right now? What are my thoughts about this situation? How am I reacting to the situation? Is it positive or am I thinking past thoughts of negativity?* Don't be upset with yourself; just stop and reroute the thinking to focus on the new goals.

Focus on what you want to attract, and radiate happiness out into the world. When you ask for what you want, visualize, and are grateful every day, the energy you put out will flow back to you. When you think about things and behave in ways that are good for you and good for the community and world, you'll receive abundance.

When you're a greedy, selfish person who doesn't care about anyone else, you can still get what you want, but trust that it will come with a great big price tag.

How are you going to use your mind? What will you attract? What kind of thoughts do you need to think to bring balance to all areas of your life? Now that you know how to use the power of the law of attraction, you know that you can realize your dreams. I'm so excited for you, and I look forward to hearing your success stories.

Bridge the Gap Between the Law of Attraction and Inspired Action

We make
A LIVING
by what
we get,
we make

by what
we give.

- Author Unknown

CHAPTER 15

Community and Giving

Many of us are so bogged down with the struggles of daily life that we don't spend any time thinking about the importance of giving back or belonging to a larger community. We may have strong and meaningful connections with our close friends and the people in our immediate family, but we feel very removed from our neighbors and society. In Western culture, and especially in big cities, where more and more people live each year, our personal connections are fewer than they have ever been in human history.

WHAT'S MISSING

When people are together in a group, a large majority of them looking at their phones instead of communicating with each other. We see this all day, every day. It's unnatural behavior for human beings. It's unhealthy.

We are social animals. We crave connection. The sense of belonging and caring for each other is within each person. Even if we don't fully realize it, we are incomplete without these connections. The absence of them leaves us feeling like we are missing something.

When we arrive at the place where we are balanced and living in abundance, we gain the capacity to give to others. When we are filled with gratitude, we can have compassion for others who need our love and support. Giving to others—whether it's attention, time, resources, reputation, material goods, or money—is essential to living a fuller, happier, more successful, and more meaningful life. When you help and connect with another person, you both win.

A LITTLE LOVE EVERY DAY

Helping others and giving is more than just doing things for people who are less fortunate. It's noble to participate in efforts to alleviate the suffering of others who are hungry, homeless, or living in poverty. But at some point in their life, every single person, even those who are more successful than you, needs love or help. Your act of kindness, large or small, can make a tremendous difference in a moment or throughout the life of another person.

Being kind also make you happier, and the happier you are, the more people you are able to help and enable to make others happy. When you do something nice for another person, that person is more likely to behave that way to the next person. It's a beautiful chain reaction and something you can do right now, for free.

You might be thinking, *I don't have enough time or money to do anything for anyone; I'm barely hanging on myself.* You do. Having empathy and encouraging another person can be as simple as allowing yourself to be vulnerable for a moment. Make eye contact with the people you encounter and smile. They might not smile back, and that's OK.

You are only responsible for your decisions and actions. You can't control how anyone else will behave. But most of the time you will see that the other person lights up a little when you give them a small amount of true consideration and send your positive vibes toward them.

You can make a mental decision to be kind to people you know and to the people you meet every single day. You are so fortunate to be able to give total strangers a gift each day. It is true that to give is better than to receive. Feelings of sadness, loneliness, regret, and want dissipate when they are replaced with feelings of love, generosity, and being empowered.

HELLO, NEIGHBOR

Start with your neighborhood. How many of your neighbors do you know? Wouldn't it be wonderful to be connected to the people who live around us? These are the people who are our second set of eyes when packages are delivered, who help us find the cat that got out, who we can turn to in an emergency for a ride, or who can help us celebrate our lives.

If you're considering having a yard sale, why not knock on the doors of the next few neighbors and invite them to join? If you're having a big party, ask them to be a part of it. The next time you're baking cookies, bake the neighbors a few and bring them by.

Every Halloween, we put two big tables out in our driveway filled with wine, a keg of beer, fruits, a water cooler, and virgin Jell-O shots. We play "monster" music and the entire neighborhood stops by to join our party. You cannot imagine how happy it makes people to be part of this night; it creates a tighter-knit community and brings everyone a feeling of contentment.

Every election we see political signs all over people's yards, and we see reminders to pick up dog poop and drive like our kids live there. What would our neighborhoods be like if our signs said SMILE, EVERYTHING IS GOING TO BE ALL RIGHT! or IT'S OK IF WE HAVE DIFFERENT BELIEFS—I STILL WANT TO BE YOUR FRIEND! or YOU ARE LOOKING ABSOLUTELY FABULOUS TODAY!

We don't have to put these signs up, but we can carry these messages around with our speech and our actions. If society is disconnected, sick, unhappy, and unwell, and this is surrounding you, how happy can you be? Whether it's on your street or around the globe, we need to interact with and support each other.

WHAT YOU HAVE TO GIVE

So far in this book, we've explored what we have to give others in the Relationships Quadrant of our life. We took a detailed look at what brings us meaning and purpose in our work and in the Finances Quadrant. We've examined how we are able to practice self-care and love in our Wellness Quadrant.

Hopefully by this part of the book you are starting to understand how much you have to give and what your unique strengths are that can make a change in someone else's life. You may witness other people who are charitable and think, *I'm nothing like that. Those people give so much time or money; I'm not able to do that.* That is their journey.

You have your own blessings to share, and they are just as valuable to the person or community who needs them. Don't wait until the day you have enough money to become engaged with others. Do it now. It can be a donation of time or money, big or small. Don't forget that time can sometimes be more valuable than money when it comes to giving. Here's a list of some things you can do to help others.

Vacation

There are so many organizations that take groups of people on charitable mission vacations. They travel to places all over the world and help communities build homes, waterways, schools, recreation centers, and other needed structures. It's a wonderful way to visit places you might never go and experience the culture in an authentic way as you work, eat, and rejoice side by side with the locals.

Speaker

You can volunteer to talk to middle or high school students about your career or share an inspirational story about something that helped you get through a tough time.

Board Member

If you have skills and knowledge in a particular field, you could offer your services as a board member for a nonprofit, helping that organization accomplish its mission.

Mentor

Whether helping to guide someone down the path you have already traveled or giving someone a person in their corner when they have no one, being a mentor is one of the most fulfilling things you will ever do.

Volunteer

The possibilities are endless. Pet adoption, working a blood drive, serving food to people in need on a holiday; the joy you receive is immeasurable. I taught two adults how to read through my local library reading program. Then they each taught two other people, and so on. My relatively small contribution is echoing through my community and changing so many lives for the better.

Open Your Door

If you know a person (and maybe their family) at work or school who has nowhere to go on a holiday, invite them to share your table.

Gifts

How many of you don't need any more stuff, but the birthday rolls around and people feel obligated to bring a gift to your birthday party? It's perfectly fine to ask for donations to a cause that you care about in lieu of gifts. My twelve- and fourteen-year-old nephews did that on their birthdays and started a trend of giving among their teenage friends.

Money

Some of us are better at making money and have very limited time, and that's great too because organizations need money. Donate money, a scholarship, or a building. But if you're just giving money to influence others to do something for you, like funding a political campaign or giving money so you can get a favor, don't delude yourself. That's not charity, that's not giving to the community—that's a bribe, and probably a crime. It probably won't give you that warm, fuzzy feeling I'm talking about.

Influence

Do you know someone who can help an organization or a person? Do you have a relationship with a company who would be willing to donate products or supplies to a school or group? Do you have a powerful friend or contact who can solve a problem or unclog a bottleneck?

Do you know both someone who is looking for a new job and someone else who could help him or her? Putting these people in touch with each other, because of your connections to each of them, is a form of giving.

Shelter

If a disaster like a fire, flood, or hurricane has occurred and you have a vacation home or guesthouse, you could offer it for temporary housing for a family who has lost everything.

Vote with Your Dollar

Buy from companies who give to others, or take care of their employees or the environment. The shoe company Toms is a perfect example. You buy a pair of shoes and they give a pair to a kid who needs one.

I don't like wearing those shoes (I think they are ugly and they hurt my feet). But I sure do buy them as gifts for the people I know who like wearing them. Are there companies you can buy from that support causes you care about?

Airline Miles

You can donate miles to charities like the Red Cross or Make-A-Wish. These organizations fly sick people and their families to places where they can receive treatment, or send terminally ill children to visit Disneyland before they die. We've all got a few thousand miles sitting around that we'll never use on some random airline. Google donating airline miles if this sounds appealing to you.

Closets

Clean out your closet, removing the clutter of items you will never wear again, and donate to Dress for Success. Someone will benefit tremendously by receiving something you don't want or need. Showing up to an interview in a new-to-them outfit can instill the confidence that someone needs to land their dream job.

Give Up Your Seat

Maybe you just get up. Offer your coveted aisle seat to a family that couldn't get seats together on the train, bus, or plane.

Small Acts Matter Too

Everyday simple acts are a form of giving that you can accomplish every time you leave the house. You can really change the world by consistently being kind and helpful to others. Whenever I go to the beach, I pick up ten pieces of trash. People see me doing this, with trash that is obviously not mine, and then they start picking up trash. It keeps trash out of our ocean and we all feel like we are a part of something bigger, even though we only exchange a nod.

It's even more granular than that. You can remember to always say please and thank you, even when you're mad. Smile at others instead of looking away.

Don't look down at your phone or text while people are talking to you. Have a little more patience for someone who is slow to cross the street. Pay a compliment to a stranger. Give your house-keeper flowers for no reason. Put a sticker on your car that says something that makes people laugh. Move around this planet with the intention to connect and give to others.

When you behave this way you strengthen communities, making people become aware of each other. You might open up a dialogue that would have never happened, or alleviate another person's suffering. You could be the catalyst in someone else's life that pushes them out of repeated failure and into success. You could heal your own pain by helping others to heal.

This whole book is about how you can feel happier, how you can accomplish your financial goals, be healthy, be mindful, and be successful. You have to care about other people; you cannot skip this part and be whole.

We need human connection; we need to see good in the world. Whether it's a small thing or a sweeping gesture, every day offers you a chance to affect someone's life. Embrace that power and use it to make a difference.

Community

Worrying
is like
praying
for something
that you
don't want
to happen.

– Robert Downey Jr.

CHAPTER 16

Overcoming Fear

Having fear is healthy and normal. The feelings and corresponding physical responses of being afraid are wired in us for survival. We think of fear as being weak because we are taught to be positive.

We've been told "There's nothing to be afraid of" since we were very little. Some fears are very real and you shouldn't ignore them. Fear is natural, and in some situations it can be very helpful. If you feel anxiety about not getting a project done on time, your fear could be the thing that keeps you from being fired. If you are afraid of being late, these feelings are what keep you from missing a flight.

You may keep yourself out of harm's way by choosing not to go to a place that is deemed to be dangerous. When you're hiking someplace steep, your fear tells you to stay away from the edge. Maybe you're presented with a financial opportunity, but you fear your investment will be lost because something just doesn't feel right.

You might be dating someone who has told you about how they cheated on their partners in the past. Your fear that this could happen to you might encourage you to stop dating them and save yourself some heartache. Could your fears be an indication of what you should or should not do? Is there something you can learn from your fears? Pay attention to them and validate whether or not they are justified.

SCARY STORIES

You'll find that many of our fears are unfounded. They are manufactured into scenarios that are grossly magnified and distorted versions of imagined outcomes. Most of our fears are merely negative thoughts that we keep running over and over again in our minds.

> *I will never find a partner who will love me.*
> *I am never going to make enough money to get myself out*
> *   of debt.*
> *I will never become the person I want to be.*
> *I will never get fit, so I'll just stop trying.*
> *I always make bad choices and I will always fail.*
> *I'm afraid of missing out.*
> *I'm afraid of the dark.*
> *I'm never going to get better.*

Sometimes we make up the worst stories and use our imagination to fill in the blanks. The more fear we feel, the more afraid we become. What if you could use that same storytelling ability to tell yourself a story that is more powerful than your fear? What if you could look at that fear, face it, and learn how to overcome it? You can.

You just need to identify your fear. Once you understand something, you can deal with it. It's not always your fault that you feel afraid, but it is always your decision how you will deal with those feelings.

GETTING UNSTUCK

When we are afraid, our body and brain go into the sympathetic nervous system state of fight, flight, or freeze. When we need it the most, our brain slows down the problem-solving areas. Fear can put you into a temporary or prolonged state of paralysis. It's the modern version of freezing in place so a predator won't see you.

When you can't make a decision that you need to make because you're afraid of the outcome, it's called analysis paralysis. Going over and over and over and over with the same thoughts and questions will not change the situation. What it might do is give you a stomachache, insomnia, self-doubt, insecurity, distrust, or panic that can spin into full-blown depression, paranoia, and hatred.

Reaching beyond the fear by moving your mind back to a calm, parasympathetic state is going to ignite the problem-solving parts of your brain. This will help you create ideas of how you move forward. Sometimes we are so stuck in this paralysis that we forget we are in control, and fear spirals into unhealthy anxiety. When levels of fear and anxiety get so high that they interfere with your ability to do what you need to do, it's time to address the underlying issues of fear.

If you feel like you are incapable of dealing with this on your own, there is no shame in talking to someone. You can work with a life coach, a trusted friend, or even a therapist. Alone or with help, when you name the fear and address ways to handle it or move past it, you can begin to grow, make sound choices, and become balanced.

LEANING INTO FEAR

Understand that there is a difference between being uncomfortable and being afraid. If you are uncomfortable about making a change where you will have to do things differently, learn new skills, or meet new people, that's normal. If you get to a place where you are so afraid that you won't be able to make those changes, that's not so good.

When you're faced with apprehension about a situation, ask yourself: what's the issue? *What's the worst thing that can happen? What can I do to overcome that thing?* We're wired to avoid things that are painful or have the potential to hurt us. That's not a bad thing when we could actually get hurt from those things, but it's stifling when the fear is irrational.

If we explore our fear and work out the possibilities, we can usually see there are other ways to think. Knowing there are acceptable options can help us gain the perspective to realize it's not as bad as we think it might be. Sometimes it's really helpful to write the fear down, listing the worst-case scenarios and what you can do to mitigate them. The act of writing forces you to take action and get out of your head.

IDENTIFYING WITH OTHERS

Sometimes it's good to do some research online and see how others are dealing with the same thing. Has anyone else ever figured out how to deal with this? What did they do? You can turn paranoia into preparation so you are ready if any of your fears actually do come true. When you are prepared for the worst, you can deal with anything.

One of the most inspiring examples of this is what happened to my aunt when she found out she had breast cancer. Immediately she thought about the possible outcomes.

- She could be cured quickly with minimal distress to her body and mind.
- She might have to go through chemotherapy. Her hair could fall out. Her breast might have to be cut off.
- Death was even a consideration.

Knowing she didn't want to do chemotherapy, she found the best doctors who performed radiation treatment. Her affairs were put in order in case the very worst scenario occurred.

Instead of being consumed by fear, she knew she needed to be positive and set up an action plan to deal with all the possible outcomes. Having concrete plans to deal with the unknown freed up space in her mind to send healing thoughts to her body. When people asked her if she was afraid, she said, "No, I am sure I will be fine. There's no reason for cancer to be in my body. I will be healthy."

There's no doubt in my mind that her ability to face her fear and move right through it helped her get well rapidly. She has been a pillar of strength for me throughout my life, and whenever I feel afraid of anything, I think of how she dealt with cancer.

THINKING IT THROUGH

When you are afraid, identify the fear and the damage it might cause. Come up with strategies to lessen or avoid that damage. More often than not, going through this process reveals that the fear did not warrant so much attention. You also learn how effective you can be in a crisis.

Sometimes we overestimate the outcome of a fear. We think the bad thing is going to be so insurmountable that we will never be able to recover from it. Our thoughts are not even necessarily the truth—we just imagine some horrid outcome as the fear grows in our mind. The chances of the thing we are imagining happening are highly unlikely, but we give themit the attention of an immediate and real danger.

My daughter had a burning sensation on her head yesterday and she became concerned that something was very wrong. She asked me if I knew what was going on, and I had no idea. I suggested that we could look it up by researching her symptoms on the internet.

She immediately said, "No! I don't want to learn that I have brain cancer." That's how fast your mind is able to go from fear to a made-up story that makes you more afraid than you need to be. I was pretty confident that she didn't have brain cancer, so I looked up the symptoms for brain cancer and started reading them out loud.

Learning that she had none of those symptoms gave her the confidence to recalibrate her fears. She reconsidered and thought it was probably just something that bit her or irritated her skin. She decided to wash and condition her hair. She felt better after doing that.

THE WHAT-IFS

Have you ever been in a situation where you conjure up some terrible thing that is going to happen and you start thinking, *I'm never going to be able move past this*? Do you start having feelings of loss before you have lost anything?

It could be something like, *If I stop working at this horrible job, I will lose my health insurance, my friends, my ability to make money.* Other jobs have these same benefits.

If I go on a diet, I won't be able eat pizza and brownies anymore. Maybe you can eat those things if they are made in a healthier way.

If I stop drinking, I won't have any fun. Maybe you'll have more fun if you're not hungover and making a fool of yourself when you're wasted.

If I break up with this person, no one else will make feel good. Someone else will make you feel better if you allow that to happen.

Every time you dive into unreasonable fears, you feed those fears and make them stronger. Tell yourself: *This is just fear. I really don't have to listen to this. I'm going to focus on finding solutions or just take a break from these thoughts.*

THE WISDOM OF EXPERIENCE

Can you use your past experiences to help face your fears? Was there ever a time that you were afraid and the fears turned out to be unwarranted? Or you were scared to do something, but you did it and you succeeded?

Give attention to the feelings you had when you beat your fears. You will muster the self-assurance to feel like you can do it again. You don't need to wish fears away, or not feel them. Acknowledge the temporary feeling of discomfort, and instead of being crippled by the fear, summon the courage to tell yourself that you will be OK.

The fear may linger in the back of your mind, but in the front is the belief that you will prevail, no matter what. Face your fear and take action in spite of it. Give focus to the thing you want to happen, not what you are afraid will happen. Remember how the power of attraction works.

FAILURE IS POSSIBLE

What if I do the work, I pass through the fear, and the outcome isn't what I wanted? It's possible that you'll identify your fear, face your fear, and still wind up failing.

Have this ever happened to you before?

Have you ever been afraid, took action and failed, and then said, "I knew this would happen!" How bad did it make you feel? How long did it last? Were you able to pick yourself up and move forward? Probably.

Does it feel worse when you have failed or does it feel better when you have succeeded? This is part of identifying and preparing for the worst-case scenario. You begin to understand that failure is not the end of the world. It might not feel great, but you will survive.

You can let your fears stop you from trying. You can keep ruminating in your mind about things that make you afraid. Or you can realize that experiencing fear can be a short-term feeling that you can overcome.

When you are ready to succeed, you will accept the fact that you are able to face your fear and move right past it to a state of action or acceptance. Separate what you can control from what you cannot, and focus only on what you can control. You have everything you need to conquer fear by planting seeds of confidence in your mind.

Conclusion

You've made it to the last chapter. Whew! That was a lot of information. You want balance in your life and you took action to get it. Congratulations, that's one of those little wins for you!

YOUR COMPASS

Living a full, successful, happy, and balanced life is all about those two things: wanting something that's good for you and taking the necessary action to get it. I wish I could say that after reading this book one time, your life will be balanced and easy going forward without having to do anything else. But we both know that is not true. This book is not magic, and you will not transform overnight by reading it. It is a compass to your true north.

Whenever you feel out of balance, you can always go back to the relevant parts of this book and get re-centered. There are thousands of moving parts in your life. It's asking a lot of yourself to be able to remember all the different things you need to be thinking and doing well, every second of your life. You can't always be monitoring every thought you have.

The aim is to be aware, not perfect. That means when you find yourself doing something that's the opposite of what you read in this book, you must be aware of it. That will be a reminder that you need to get back on course.

Being in balance is a lifelong practice of making adjustments and getting back in alignment. Take action, and don't be afraid to reroute. Even while writing this book, I found myself having small setbacks, making mistakes, feeling out of control, being afraid, and losing my temper. I had to go back and reread my own words so that I could start over.

Like you, I'm not perfect all day, every day. What is important is that I was aware of my behavior and how it immediately made me feel off balance. I responded to myself with patience and forgiveness, then altered my actions or thoughts to get back on track. That's exactly what I want you to do when you get out of balance.

MAKING BETTER MOVES

Everyone is different. Each one of us has a unique idea about what being in balance means. Ask yourself: why are you doing the things you do? What is important to you? What can you do to align what you're doing with what is important to you?

No matter what has happened to you in your past, or what mistakes you have made in your life, you have the chance, starting right now, to make new choices. You have the power to stop allowing destructive thoughts and patterns that you picked up in the past to negatively affect your life and relationships. The decision to be in positive relationships with people who lift you up is yours. Spending time nurturing these connections is an investment that pays priceless dividends.

If someone consistently makes you feel bad, and there's no possible resolution, you must let him or her go, even if they are family. You have worth and you don't allow others to diminish you. Surround yourself with people you admire, people you love, and people who feel the same way about you.

You know how to find them. You know how to avoid the wrong people. Trust your gut, and when in doubt, ask for a friend or family member's opinion.

FINANCIAL FOUNDATIONS

Being in balance means being happy. Money can't buy you happiness, but you will be very unhappy if you do not manage your finances. You have got to pay attention to this area of your life and develop a financial IQ.

Spend time thinking about your goals and how you can take realistic steps to achieve them. Realize that your happiness and success in life is not dictated by what others say you should have. You don't need to "keep up with the Joneses" to feel successful.

When possible, avoid listening to commercials and reading advertisements. They are literally a form of brainwashing that coerces you into buying things you don't need.

Something else you don't need is a job or career that makes you miserable. Your time is too precious to waste doing something that doesn't fulfill you or threatens your well-being. There are so many ways to make a living that will resonate with your beliefs, talents, and desires. Adjust your plans when they don't work for you. Use your previous experiences to craft a new beginning.

BEING WELL

Having harmonious relationships and financial security provides a rock-solid foundation for your balancing act. But if you don't feel well, you won't perform well. Without mental and physical wellness, you cannot achieve success. The whole point of being balanced is feeling centered, feeling whole, and feeling like you can tackle any challenge.

Wellness doesn't mean you have to be in top model shape. It means being healthy in your mind and your body. Take care of yourself. Eat things that nourish your body. Experiment with different types of food to find things that taste good and are good for you. They do exist.

Move, stretch, and breathe vitality into your system every day. Create an environment that allows you to sleep deeply and for enough hours. Remember to pamper yourself, daily or weekly, doing things to rejuvenate your body and mind.

GRATITUDE AND COURAGE

Finding balance in relationships, finances, and wellness all begins and ends with your spirituality. If you're moving in a direction that is good and good for others, there is a force that propels you to be able to take the first step and keeps you moving forward. Some people think it's a connection to the Universe, karma, or even quantum physics.

The first step in the right direction of a better life could be the hardest one to take. You might even feel paralyzed, unable to move. It's your spirituality that gives you the confidence to take that step. Put one foot in front of the other and watch the doors open.

Practice gratitude. Slow down. Be quiet. Listen. Be in the moment. Give whatever you can to others. Do the right thing, even when no one is watching. Practice the way you want to play. If you get distracted and lose confidence, energy, or focus, go back to your core beliefs and inner strength.

Everyone is afraid sometimes. Fear is the number-one reason people don't find balance. They are afraid of not being enough, not being loved, or failing. I promise you that if you try new things, you will fail sometimes. That's OK. When you fail, remember a time when you survived, a time when you succeeded because you pushed through. Then, do that again. Forgive yourself for not being perfect. Forgive yourself when you fall short.

Think, speak, and act in ways that expand your potential and don't diminish you or others. Think about your twelve-year-old self. Would she or he be proud of you? Don't give any credence to people who put you down or try to hold you back. Do not be the person who puts others down.

In our world of digital interaction, remember that there are real people who have real feelings on the other side of the nasty comments and reviews. If you have nothing nice to say and your comments aren't going to help someone, don't leave them. Use your power, time, resources, and influence to lift others up, not tear them down.

Before I wrap this up, I want to introduce you to my friend KariAnne Wood. In addition to being an award-winning blogger and author of two bestselling books, *You've Got This (Because God's Got You)* and *So Close to Amazing*, she is one of the most authentic people I have ever met. This lady understands that belonging isn't about changing to fit in, but instead celebrating exactly who you are and sharing it with others. She lets her freak flag fly. You can't help but love her.

KariAnne realizes that in order to be successful, you have to be vulnerable and face your fears. The first day I met her, she shared this story with me about doing something new and scary. I know it will inspire you to go for it, whatever it is!

Several years ago, when my blog was still learning to walk, I decided to attend a blogging conference. I went solo. *All alone.* All by myself without any peeps.

The first night of the conference began with a cocktail party for all the attendees. I put on a brand-new outfit, teased my highlighted hair to the sky, and walked my blinged-out-flip-flop self downstairs and into a dark room filled with people I had never met before in my entire life.

Wide-eyed, I entered the room, clutching my homemade business cards that I had printed off at Wal-Mart. *You know.* The kind with the perforated edges still attached. With a smile and a confident toss of my brilliantly coiffed hair, I walked up to the first group of bloggers I saw.

They asked me my blog name. I handed them my business card with an optimistic smile and waited for the fun to start. This is the part of the story where we were all going to hug and talk blogging and give each other ideas and hold hands and become best friends forever.

Maybe not.

Maybe not even close. They didn't want to be friends. Not even a little. They looked at each other with a look that spoke volumes. A look that said that they had never heard of me. Then they gave me a cursory glance and looked over my head to see if someone more popular was around.

Really?

I stood there awkwardly for a moment as my hair and my outstretched business card wilted just a little. And then, undaunted, I soldiered on. I approached another group of beautiful people laughing and talking and becoming instant best friends . . . *and it happened again.*

And again. And again. *And again.*

I reached out and tried to fit in. I tried to make friends until my confidence was shattered. Until inside I shivered. Until I wanted to take my earrings and flip-flops and my business cards and run all the way home. *Instead?* I gathered my tattered pride and my bedraggled hair and left with my head held high. I went up to my hotel room and sat and on my bed and cried.

Tears fell on my phone as it beeped. Flipping it up, I listened to a voicemail from my children. They were calling to wish me luck. They wanted to ask me how much fun I was having and to hear the stories about all the new friends I had met.

sigh

That voicemail made me cry harder. It made me wish I had ordered my business cards from a fancy online store. It made me wish my blog was funnier and brighter and more creative and . . . *and* . . . *and* . . . just better.

And then I stopped mid-pity party. What was I doing? What was I thinking? Why was I worried about my blog being better or more creative or funnier or more than it was?

I was there. *KariAnne.*

Seriously. *I was in the house.* I showed up. I was at the conference with my stories and my waving hands and my giggle and my joy. And me, myself, and I were better than any blog could ever hope to be.

And so it was that the next day I marched myself downstairs with a sparkling set of flip-flops and a new attitude and then I laughed and danced and listened and storied my way through the conference. Maybe it was the flip-flops.

Maybe it was the new perspective. Maybe it was the joy bubbling out of me for the next forty-eight hours.

Whatever the reason, on the last day of the conference I sat on the front row and appointed myself to approach the sponsors and thank them for hosting the event. Like I was on the greeting committee. Like I was someone important—someone with a voice to be heard and a story to tell.

Someone amazing.

Just like me.

PS: Five years later, I was the keynote speaker at the event. See? Amazing triumphs every time.

If you can be open-minded and use the information in this book to find balance in your life, you will be happy. What's better than being happy? Nothing. Because when you are happy, everything that you need will come to you in the amount that you can handle. In the words of my friend KariAnne, "You got this."

Index

 **Books from Allworth Press**

Boost Your Career
by Sander and Mechele Flaum (5½ × 8¼, 208 pages, paperback, $16.99)

The Creative Path
by Carolyn Schlam (6 × 9, 256 pages, paperback, $19.99)

Feng Shui and Money (Second Edition)
by Eric Shaffert (6 × 9, 256 pages, paperback, $19.99)

Fund Your Dreams Like a Creative Genius™
by Brainard Carey (6⅛ × 6⅛, 160 pages, paperback, $12.99)

Green Interior Design (Second Edition)
by Lori Dennis (8½ × 10, 160 pages, paperback, $24.99)

Intentional Leadership
by Jane A. G. Kise (7 × 10, 224 pages, paperback, $19.95)

Learning by Heart (Second Edition)
by Corita Kent and Jan Steward (7 × 9⅛, 232 pages, paperback, $24.95)

Love & Money
by Ann-Margaret Carrozza with foreword by Dr. Phil McGraw (6 × 9, 240 pages, paperback, $19.99)

The Money Mentor
by Tad Crawford (6 × 9, 272 pages, paperback, $24.95)

Unfolding Self
by Molly Young Brown (6 × 9, 240 pages, paperback, $17.95)

To see our complete catalog or to order online, please visit *www.allworth.com*.